The definitive
management ideas
of the year from
Harvard Business Review.

2017

HBR's 10 Must Reads series is the definitive collection of ideas and best practices for aspiring and experienced leaders alike. These books offer essential reading selected from the pages of *Harvard Business Review* on topics critical to the success of every manager.

Titles include:

HBR's 10 Must Reads 2015
HBR's 10 Must Reads 2016
HBR's 10 Must Reads 2017
HBR's 10 Must Reads on Change Management
HBR's 10 Must Reads on Collaboration
HBR's 10 Must Reads on Communication
HBR's 10 Must Reads on Emotional Intelligence
HBR's 10 Must Reads on Innovation
HBR's 10 Must Reads on Leadership
HBR's 10 Must Reads on Making Smart Decisions
HBR's 10 Must Reads on Managing Across Cultures
HBR's 10 Must Reads on Managing People
HBR's 10 Must Reads on Managing Yourself
HBR's 10 Must Reads on Strategic Marketing
HBR's 10 Must Reads on Strategy
HBR's 10 Must Reads on Teams
HBR's 10 Must Reads: The Essentials

The definitive
management ideas
of the year from
Harvard Business Review.

2017

HARVARD BUSINESS REVIEW PRESS
Boston, Massachusetts

Copyright 2017 Harvard Business School Publishing Corporation
All rights reserved
Printed in the United States of America
10 9 8 7 6 5 4 3 2 1

No part of this publication may be reproduced, stored in or introduced into a retrieval system, or transmitted, in any form, or by any means (electronic, mechanical, photocopying, recording, or otherwise), without the prior permission of the publisher. Requests for permission should be directed to permissions@hbsp.harvard.edu, or mailed to Permissions, Harvard Business School Publishing, 60 Harvard Way, Boston, Massachusetts 02163.

The web addresses referenced in this book were live and correct at the time of book's publication but may be subject to change.

Cataloging-in-Publication data is forthcoming.

ISBN: 978-1-63369-209-1
eISBN: 978-1-63369-210-7

The paper used in this publication meets the requirements of the American National Standard for Permanence of Paper for Publications and Documents in Libraries and Archives Z39.48-1992.

Contents

Editors' Note

"People are the ultimate source of sustainable competitive differentiation," write Ram Charan, Dominic Barton, and Dennis Carey in their article "People Before Strategy: A New Role for the CHRO." But it may not always be so. Take the growing tension between man and machine: To what extent will knowledge workers' jobs be replaced by smart products? What is the role of a human professional in a world of big data and predictive algorithms?

In this volume we showcase this and other critical themes highlighted by our authors from the past year of *Harvard Business Review*. Many of these articles stress the continued need to elevate employees' work to new levels and unleash their innovative energy. Our authors explore big trends in business—like the increased focus on collaboration and empathy—that emphasize distinctly human skills. Executives and academics alike reengage with design thinking, explaining how to build products, processes, and platforms around users' experiences. Other authors highlight the need to retool models and metrics for a world where human interactions have become the major source of value. All these ideas highlight that even as technology marches forward, human knowledge and expertise remain critical to strategy and performance.

We begin this collection with a piece that studies how individuals work together. Collaboration has become a hot topic in recent years, and indeed it offers organizations a host of benefits. But it also poses risks: The most productive contributors often burn out from carrying the weight of their teams. In **"Collaborative Overload,"** professors and researchers Rob Cross, Reb Rebele, and Adam Grant present practical ways to manage collaboration effectively—by redistributing work evenly and rewarding efficient efforts—for high performance without exhaustion.

Like collaboration, big data provides organizations with tremendous opportunity—but also has its limitations. In **"Algorithms Need Managers, Too,"** professors Michael Luca, Jon Kleinberg, and Sendhil Mullainathan explain what questions algorithms can—and can't—answer, so companies will be able to use them more effectively. While algorithms can identify patterns in data and generate insights at incredible speed and scale, the authors illustrate, through examples from Netflix movie recommendations to Google ads, how algorithms can also produce unintended consequences if designed too literally or without accounting for all critical goals. It takes managerial know-how to clarify cause and effect, identify risks, and make important decisions.

Our next piece, **"Pipelines, Platforms, and the New Rules of Strategy,"** redefines strategic advantage. For years managers have relied on Michael Porter's five forces model of competition. But with platform businesses such as Uber and Alibaba, the distinctions among the forces are less clear, and new competitive factors come into play. It's now imperative to understand "network effects"—to facilitate interactions between consumers and producers, and to incorporate those interactions into metrics of success. In this article professors Marshall W. Van Alstyne and Geoffrey G. Parker and executive adviser Sangeet Paul Choudary explain the new keys to competitive advantage and how traditional pipeline companies can develop the core competencies to survive in a platform world.

Porter's five forces isn't the only classic management concept to be reexamined in HBR this year. Two decades ago Clayton M. Christensen introduced the theory of disruptive innovation, but since then, journalists, researchers, and business practitioners have misinterpreted its concepts and misapplied its principles. Uber, for instance, has been highlighted as a shining star of disruption, but does it truly fit the definition? In **"What Is Disruptive Innovation?"** Christensen and his coauthors, Michael Raynor and Rory McDonald, provide a primer on the theory, explain how it has evolved, and correct common misperceptions. Their article will help managers to understand how firms innovate successfully and to predict which new models will succeed.

The next piece is an interview with a top business leader: **"How Indra Nooyi Turned Design Thinking into Strategy."** HBR editor-in-chief Adi Ignatius asks the CEO of PepsiCo hard-hitting questions about how the company is using design to improve products and customer experiences. Moving beyond the basics of color choice on labels, Pepsi has examined how different segments of its customer base are responding to and using its products. Nooyi's story is less of a tale of product design, however, and more about managing change in an organization while creating a platform that encourages customer interaction.

Identifying and understanding the needs of customers—this time, consumers in the developing world—is a key element of Amos Winter and Vijay Govindarajan's McKinsey Award-winning article, **"Engineering Reverse Innovations."** In 2009, Govindarajan first described the concept of "reverse innovation," in which Western multinationals create products and services for emerging markets *first* and then export them to developed countries. This article explains how to escape the five traps companies often fall into while attempting to innovate for the developing world, drawing on the experiences of a team that built a successful low-priced wheelchair.

The cost of goods may be a major concern in poorer countries, but for companies in the United States, the amount spent on health care is even more challenging. **"The Employer-Led Health Care Revolution,"** by Patricia A. McDonald, Robert S. Mecklenburg, and Lindsay A. Martin, describes how Intel and a health care institution teamed up to transform the local health care system. By using its purchasing power and working directly with care providers, health plan administrators, insurers, and other employers, Intel was able to streamline health care operations, creating low-cost options for both employers and patients. In this article the authors identify the ingredients of this successful experiment, in the hope that other large employers can follow its example.

Negotiations are an everyday event in business, whether they're about prices from a vendor or schedules for clients. But when they take place between people from different cultures, the dynamics become much more complex and miscommunication is more common. It's all too easy to damage relationships irreversibly. Our next piece, **"Getting to *Sí, Ja, Oui, Hai,* and *Da*"** by INSEAD professor Erin Meyer, provides five rules of thumb for negotiating across cultures. From building trust with your counterpart to understanding the subtle messages in emotional outbursts, Meyer's advice illuminates how to strike the right balance and reach that final agreement—and make it stick.

Empathy—the art of understanding others' needs and responding with compassion—is essential to motivating colleagues, calming upset customers, and designing innovative products. But frequent demands for empathy can exhaust your workers—and even cause them to make unethical decisions. In **"The Limits of Empathy,"** Adam Waytz of the Kellogg School of Management suggests simple strategies to encourage your team to empathize in a more healthy, sustainable way.

"Businesses don't create value; people do" is a popular adage among CEOs—but often those same CEOs are dissatisfied with the human resource officers who manage the organization's workforce. In **"People Before Strategy: A New Role for the CHRO,"** business advisers Ram Charan, Dominic Barton, and Dennis Carey argue for a new C-level leader whose sole responsibility is to think strategically about an organization's talent—from identifying and creatively engaging high potentials to developing new performance metrics that better support business goals. This piece provides practical ideas on how to implement this change and ensure that people remain the ultimate source of competitive advantage.

The last article in this volume takes us back to the tension between man and machine. **"Beyond Automation,"** by Thomas H. Davenport and Julia Kirby, taps into the fear many white-collar employees feel as new technologies make more jobs obsolete. The authors assert that human employees will still be necessary in the future—but they'll have to find ways to proactively partner with machines. The article identifies five ways humans can thrive at work in the future.

Despite all the amazing advances new digital tools have brought, people still matter. Businesses need individuals who can exercise intuition and judgment, who can see the gaps in data, who can assess new ideas. Most of all, they need leaders who can inspire employees and set them up for success. Competitive advantage lies not in the latest smart devices but in the way we effectively combine the potential of both technology and people.

—The Editors

HBR'S 10 MUST READS

The definitive
management ideas
of the year from
Harvard Business Review.

2017

Collaborative Overload

by Rob Cross, Reb Rebele, and Adam Grant

COLLABORATION IS TAKING OVER the workplace. As business becomes increasingly global and cross-functional, silos are breaking down, connectivity is increasing, and teamwork is seen as a key to organizational success. According to data we have collected over the past two decades, the time spent by managers and employees in collaborative activities has ballooned by 50% or more.

Certainly, we find much to applaud in these developments. However, when consumption of a valuable resource spikes that dramatically, it should also give us pause. Consider a typical week in your own organization. How much time do people spend in meetings, on the phone, and responding to e-mails? At many companies the proportion hovers around 80%, leaving employees little time for all the critical work they must complete on their own. Performance suffers as they are buried under an avalanche of requests for input or advice, access to resources, or attendance at a meeting. They take assignments home, and soon, according to a large body of evidence on stress, burnout and turnover become real risks.

What's more, research we've done across more than 300 organizations shows that the distribution of collaborative work is often extremely lopsided. In most cases, 20% to 35% of value-added collaborations come from only 3% to 5% of employees. As people become known for being both capable and willing to help, they are

1

drawn into projects and roles of growing importance. Their giving mindset and desire to help others quickly enhances their performance and reputation. As a recent study led by Ning Li, of the University of Iowa, shows, a single "extra miler"—an employee who frequently contributes beyond the scope of his or her role—can drive team performance more than all the other members combined.

But this "escalating citizenship," as the University of Oklahoma professor Mark Bolino calls it, only further fuels the demands placed on top collaborators. We find that what starts as a virtuous cycle soon turns vicious. Soon helpful employees become institutional bottlenecks: Work doesn't progress until they've weighed in. Worse, they are so overtaxed that they're no longer personally effective. And more often than not, the volume and diversity of work they do to benefit others goes unnoticed, because the requests are coming from other units, varied offices, or even multiple companies. In fact, when we use network analysis to identify the strongest collaborators in organizations, leaders are typically surprised by at least half the names on their lists. In our quest to reap the rewards of collaboration, we have inadvertently created open markets for it without recognizing the costs. What can leaders do to manage these demands more effectively?

Precious Personal Resources

First, it's important to distinguish among the three types of "collaborative resources" that individual employees invest in others to create value: informational, social, and personal. *Informational* resources are knowledge and skills—expertise that can be recorded and passed on. *Social* resources involve one's awareness, access, and position in a network, which can be used to help colleagues better collaborate with one another. *Personal* resources include one's own time and energy.

These three resource types are not equally efficient. Informational and social resources can be shared—often in a single exchange—without depleting the collaborator's supply. That is, when I offer you knowledge or network awareness, I also retain it for my

Idea in Brief

The Situation

Over the past two decades, the amount of time managers and employees spend on collaborative work has ballooned. At many companies people now spend about 80% of their time in meetings or answering colleagues' requests.

The Problem

Although the benefits of collaboration are well documented, the costs often go unrecognized.

When demands for collaboration run too high or aren't spread evenly through the organization, workflow bottlenecks and employee burnout result.

The Solution

Leaders must learn to better manage collaboration in their companies by mapping supply and demand, eliminating or redistributing work, and incentivizing people to collaborate more efficiently.

own use. But an individual employee's time and energy are finite, so each request to participate in or approve decisions for a project leaves less available for that person's own work.

Unfortunately, personal resources are often the default demand when people want to collaborate. Instead of asking for specific informational or social resources—or better yet, searching in existing repositories such as reports or knowledge libraries—people ask for hands-on assistance they may not even need. An exchange that might have taken five minutes or less turns into a 30-minute calendar invite that strains personal resources on both sides of the request.

Consider a case study from a blue-chip professional services firm. When we helped the organization map the demands facing a group of its key employees, we found that the top collaborator—let's call him Vernell—had 95 connections based on incoming requests. But only 18% of the requesters said they needed more personal access to him to achieve their business goals; the rest were content with the informational and social resources he was providing. The second most connected person was Sharon, with 89 people in her network, but her situation was markedly different, and more dangerous, because 40% of them wanted more time with her—a significantly greater draw on her personal resources.

3

We find that as the percentage of requesters seeking more access moves beyond about 25, it hinders the performance of both the individual and the group and becomes a strong predictor of voluntary turnover. As well-regarded collaborators are overloaded with demands, they may find that no good deed goes unpunished.

The exhibit "In demand, yet disengaged," reflecting data on business unit line leaders across a sample of 20 organizations, illustrates the problem. People at the top center and right of the chart—that is, those seen as the best sources of information and in highest demand

In demand, yet disengaged

Data on leaders across 20 organizations shows that those regarded by colleagues as the best information sources and most desirable collaborators have the lowest engagement and career satisfaction scores, as represented by the size of their bubbles.

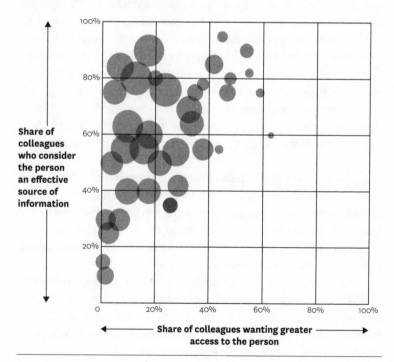

as collaborators in their companies—have the lowest engagement and career satisfaction scores, as represented by the size of their bubbles. Our research shows that this ultimately results in their either leaving their organizations (taking valuable knowledge and network resources with them) or staying and spreading their growing apathy to their colleagues.

Leaders can solve this problem in two ways: by streamlining and redistributing responsibilities for collaboration and by rewarding effective contributions.

Redistributing the Work

Any effort to increase your organization's collaborative efficiency should start with an understanding of the existing supply and demand. Employee surveys, electronic communications tracking, and internal systems such as 360-degree feedback and CRM programs can provide valuable data on the volume, type, origin, and destination of requests, as can more in-depth network analyses and tools. For example, Do.com monitors calendars and provides daily and weekly reports to both individual employees and managers about time spent in meetings versus on solo work. The idea is to identify the people most at risk for collaborative overload. Once that's been done, you can focus on three levers:

Encourage behavioral change

Show the most active and overburdened helpers how to filter and prioritize requests; give them permission to say no (or to allocate only half the time requested); and encourage them to make an introduction to someone else when the request doesn't draw on their own unique contributions. The latest version of the team-collaboration software Basecamp now offers a notification "snooze button" that encourages employees to set stronger boundaries around their incoming information flow. It's also worth suggesting that when they do invest personal resources, it be in value-added activities that they find energizing rather than exhausting. In studying employees at one *Fortune* 500 technology company, we found that although 60% wanted to spend less time responding to ad hoc collaboration requests, 40% wanted to spend more time training, coaching, and mentoring. After their contributions were shifted to those activities, employees were less prone to stress and disengagement.

To stem the tide of incoming requests, help seekers, too, must change their behavior. Resetting norms regarding when and how to initiate e-mail requests or meeting invitations can free up a great deal of wasted time. As a step in this direction, managers at Dropbox eliminated all recurring meetings for a two-week period. That forced employees to reassess the necessity of those gatherings and, after the hiatus, helped them become more vigilant about their calendars and making sure each meeting had an owner and an agenda. Rebecca Hinds and Bob Sutton, of Stanford, found that although the company tripled the number of employees at its headquarters over the next two years, its meetings were shorter and more productive.

In addition, requests for time-sapping reviews and approvals can be reduced in many risk-averse cultures by encouraging people to take courageous action on decisions they should be making themselves, rather than constantly checking with leaders or stakeholders.

Leverage technology and physical space to make informational and social resources more accessible and transparent
Relevant technical tools include Slack and Salesforce.com's Chatter, with their open discussion threads on various work topics; and Syndio and VoloMetrix (recently acquired by Microsoft), which help individuals assess networks and make informed decisions about collaborative activities. Also rethink desk or office placement. A study led by the Boston University assistant professor Stine Grodal documented the detrimental effects of team meetings and e-mails on the development and maintenance of productive helping relationships. When possible, managers should colocate highly interdependent employees to facilitate brief and impromptu face-to-face collaborations, resulting in a more efficient exchange of resources.

Consider structural changes
Can you shift decision rights to more-appropriate people in the network? It may seem obvious that support staff or lower-level

managers should be authorized to approve small capital expenditures, travel, and some HR activities, but in many organizations they aren't. Also consider whether you can create a buffer against demands for collaboration. Many hospitals now assign each unit or floor a nurse preceptor, who has no patient care responsibilities and is therefore available to respond to requests as they emerge. The result, according to research that one of us (Adam Grant) conducted with David Hofmann and Zhike Lei, is fewer bottlenecks and quicker connections between nurses and the right experts. Other types of organizations might also benefit from designating "utility players"— which could lessen demand for the busiest employees—and possibly rotating the role among team members while freeing up personal resources by reducing people's workloads.

Rewarding Effective Collaboration

We typically see an overlap of only about 50% between the top collaborative contributors in an organization and those employees deemed to be the top performers. As we've explained, many helpers underperform because they're overwhelmed; that's why managers should aim to redistribute work. But we also find that roughly 20% of organizational "stars" don't help; they hit their numbers (and earn kudos for it) but don't amplify the success of their colleagues. In these cases, as the former Goldman Sachs and GE chief learning officer Steve Kerr once wrote, leaders are hoping for A (collaboration) while rewarding B (individual achievement). They must instead learn how to spot and reward people who do both.

Consider professional basketball, hockey, and soccer teams. They don't just measure goals; they also track assists. Organizations should do the same, using tools such as network analysis, peer recognition programs, and value-added performance metrics. We helped one life sciences company use these tools to assess its workforce during a multibillion-dollar acquisition. Because the deal involved consolidating facilities around the world and relocating many employees, management was worried about losing talent. A well-known consultancy had recommended retention bonuses

Why Women Bear More of the Burden

THE LION'S SHARE OF collaborative work tends to fall on women. They're stereotyped as communal and caring, so they're expected to help others with heavy workloads, provide mentoring and training to more-junior colleagues, recruit new hires, and attend optional meetings. As a result, the evidence shows, women experience greater emotional exhaustion than men.

One important solution to this problem is to encourage women to invest different types of resources in collaboration. In a 2013 *Huffington Post* poll of Americans, men and women estimated how often they contribute to others in a variety of ways. Men were 36% more likely to share knowledge and expertise—an informational resource. Meanwhile, women were 66% more likely to assist others in need—an action that typically costs more time and energy. By making contributions that rely less on personal resources, women can protect themselves against collaboration overload.

Managers must also ensure that men and women get equal credit for collaboration. In an experiment led by the NYU psychologist Madeline Heilman, a man who stayed late to help colleagues earned 14% higher ratings than a woman who did the same. When neither helped, the woman was rated 12% lower than the man. By improving systems for measuring, recognizing, and rewarding collaborative contributions, leaders can shift the focus away from the gender of the employee and toward the value added.

for leaders. But this approach failed to consider those very influential employees deep in the acquired company who had broad impact but no formal authority. Network analytics allowed the company to pinpoint those people and distribute bonuses more fairly.

Efficient sharing of informational, social, and personal resources should also be a prerequisite for positive reviews, promotions, and pay raises. At one investment bank, employees' annual performance reviews include feedback from a diverse group of colleagues, and only those people who are rated as strong collaborators (that is, able to cross-sell and provide unique customer value to transactions) are considered for the best promotions, bonuses, and retention plans. Corning, the glass and ceramics manufacturer, uses similar metrics to decide which of its scientists and engineers will be named fellows—a high honor that guarantees a job and a lab for life. One criterion is to be the first author on a patent that generates at least $100-million in revenue. But another is whether the candidate has worked as a supporting author on colleagues' patents. Corning grants status and power to those who strike a healthy balance between individual accomplishment and collaborative contribution. (Disclosure: Adam Grant has done consulting work for Corning.)

Collaboration is indeed the answer to many of today's most pressing business challenges. But more isn't always better. Leaders must learn to recognize, promote, and efficiently distribute the right kinds of collaborative work, or their teams and top talent will bear the costs of too much demand for too little supply. In fact, we believe that the time may have come for organizations to hire chief collaboration officers. By creating a senior executive position dedicated to collaboration, leaders can send a clear signal about the importance of managing teamwork thoughtfully and provide the resources necessary to do it effectively. That might reduce the odds that the whole becomes far less than the sum of its parts.

Originally published in January–February 2016. Reprint R1601E

Algorithms Need Managers, Too

by Michael Luca, Jon Kleinberg, and Sendhil Mullainathan

MOST MANAGERS' JOBS involve making predictions. When HR specialists decide whom to hire, they're predicting who will be most effective. When marketers choose which distribution channels to use, they're predicting where a product will sell best. When VCs determine whether to fund a start-up, they're predicting whether it will succeed. To make these and myriad other business predictions, companies today are turning more and more to computer algorithms, which perform step-by-step analytical operations at incredible speed and scale.

Algorithms make predictions more accurate—but they also create risks of their own, especially if we do not understand them. High-profile examples abound. When Netflix ran a million-dollar competition to develop an algorithm that could identify which movies a given user would like, teams of data scientists joined forces and produced a winner. But it was one that applied to DVDs—and as Netflix's viewers transitioned to streaming movies, their preferences shifted in ways that didn't match the algorithm's predictions.

Another example comes from social media. Today many sites deploy algorithms to decide which ads and links to show users. When these algorithms focus too narrowly on maximizing user click-throughs, sites become choked with low-quality "click-bait" articles. Click-through rates rise, but overall customer satisfaction may plummet.

Problems like these aren't inevitable. In our work designing and implementing algorithms and identifying new data sources with a range of organizations, we have seen that the source of difficulty often isn't bugs in the algorithms; it's bugs in the way we interact with them. To avoid missteps, managers need to understand what algorithms do well—what questions they answer and what questions they do not.

Why Do Smart Algorithms Lead Us Astray?

As a growing body of evidence shows, humanizing algorithms makes us more comfortable with them. This can be useful if, for example, you're designing an automated call function. A real person's voice is more likely than an electronic voice to get people to listen. The fundamental problem, however, is that people treat algorithms and the machines that run them the same way they'd treat an employee, supervisor, or colleague. But algorithms behave very differently from humans, in two important ways:

Algorithms are extremely literal
In the latest Avengers movie, Tony Stark (also known as Iron Man) creates Ultron, an artificial-intelligence defense system tasked with protecting Earth. But Ultron interprets the task literally, concluding that the best way to save Earth is to destroy all humans. In many ways, Ultron behaves like a typical algorithm: It does exactly what it's told—and ignores every other consideration. We get into trouble when we don't manage algorithms carefully.

The social media sites that were suddenly swamped with clickbait fell into a similar trap. Their overall goal was clear: Provide content that would be most appealing and engaging to users. In communicating it to the algorithm, they came up with a set of instructions that seemed like a good proxy—find items that users will click on the most. And it's not a bad proxy: People typically click on content because it interests them. But making selections solely on

Idea in Brief

The Problem

Algorithms are essential tools for planning, but they can easily lead decision makers astray.

The Causes

All algorithms share two characteristics: They're literal, meaning that they'll do exactly what you ask them to do. And they're black

boxes, meaning that they don't explain why they offer particular recommendations.

The Solution

When formulating algorithms, be explicit about all your goals. Consider long-term implications of the data you examine. And make sure you choose the right data inputs.

---

the basis of clicks quickly filled sites with superficial and offensive material that hurt their reputation. A human would understand that the sites' designers meant "Maximize quality as measured by clicks," not "Maximize clicks even at the expense of quality." An algorithm, on the other hand, understands only what it is explicitly told.

Algorithms are black boxes

In Shakespeare's *Julius Caesar,* a soothsayer warns Caesar to "beware the ides of March." The recommendation was perfectly clear: Caesar had better watch out. Yet at the same time it was completely incomprehensible. Watch out for what? Why? Caesar, frustrated with the mysterious message, dismissed the soothsayer, declaring, "He is a dreamer; let us leave him." Indeed, the ides of March turned out to be a bad day for the ruler. The problem was that the soothsayer provided *incomplete* information. And there was no clue to what was missing or how important that information was.

Like Shakespeare's soothsayer, algorithms often can predict the future with great accuracy but tell you neither what will cause an event nor why. An algorithm can read through every *New York Times* article and tell you which is most likely to be shared on Twitter without necessarily explaining why people will be moved to tweet about it. An algorithm can tell you which employees are most likely to succeed without identifying which attributes are most important for success.

Recognizing these two limitations of algorithms is the first step to managing them better. Now let's look at other steps you can take to leverage them more successfully.

Be Explicit About All Your Goals

Everyone has objectives and directives, but we also know that the end doesn't always justify the means. We understand that there are soft (often unspoken) goals and trade-offs. We may turn down a little profit today for a gain in reputation tomorrow. We may strive for equality—even if it causes organizational pain in the short term. Algorithms, on the other hand, will pursue a specified objective single-mindedly. The best way to mitigate this is to be crystal clear about everything you want to achieve.

If you care about a soft goal, you need to state it, define it, and quantify how much it matters. To the extent that soft goals are difficult to measure, keep them top of mind when acting on the results from an algorithm.

At Google (which has funded some of our research on other topics), a soft-goal problem emerged with an algorithm that determines which ads to display. Harvard professor Latanya Sweeney unearthed it in a study. She found that when you typed names that were typically African American, like "Latanya Farrell," into Google, you were shown ads offering to investigate possible arrest records, but not when you searched on names like "Kristen Haring." Google's hard goal of maximizing clicks on ads had led to a situation in which its algorithms, refined through feedback over time, were in effect defaming people with certain kinds of names. It happened because people who searched for particular names were more likely to click on arrest records, which led these records to appear even more often, creating a self-reinforcing loop. This probably was not the intended outcome, but without a soft goal in place, there was no mechanism to steer the algorithm away from it.

We recently saw the importance of soft goals in action. One of us was working with a West Coast city to improve the efficiency of its restaurant inspections. For decades, the city had been doing them mostly at random but giving more-frequent scrutiny to places with prior violations. Choosing which establishments to inspect is an ideal job for an algorithm, however. Our algorithm found many more variables—not just past violations—to be predictive. The result was that the health department could identify probable offenders more easily and then find actual violations with far fewer inspections.

The officials loved the idea of making the process more efficient and wanted to move toward implementation. We asked if there were any questions or concerns. After an awkward silence, one person raised her hand. "I don't know how to bring this up," she said. "But there's an issue we should discuss." She explained that in some neighborhoods with tighter quarters, there tended to be more violations. These neighborhoods also happened to be home to higher percentages of minority residents with lower incomes. She did not want these neighborhoods to be excessively targeted by the algorithm. She was expressing a soft goal related to fairness. Our simple solution was to incorporate that objective into the algorithm by setting a ceiling on the number of inspections within each area. This would achieve the hard goal, identifying the restaurants most likely to have problems, while still respecting the soft one, ensuring that poor neighborhoods were not singled out.

Notice the extra step that allowed us to bake in soft goals: giving everyone an opportunity to articulate any concerns. We find that people often formulate soft goals as concerns, so asking for them explicitly facilitates more open and fruitful discussion. It's also critical to give people license to be candid and up-front—to say things that they wouldn't normally. This approach can surface a variety of issues, but the ones we see most commonly relate to fairness and to the handling of sensitive situations.

With a core objective and a list of concerns in hand, the designer of the algorithm can then build trade-offs into it. Often that may mean extending the objective to include multiple outcomes, weighted by importance.

Minimize Myopia

A popular consumer packaged goods company was purchasing products cheaply in China and selling them in the United States. It selected these products after running an algorithm that forecast which ones would sell the most. Sure enough, sales took off and cruised along nicely—until several months later, when customers started to return the items.

As it happens, the surprisingly high and steady return rate could have been predicted (even though the algorithm had failed to foresee it). The company obviously cared about quality, but it hadn't translated that interest into an algorithm that carefully projected consumer satisfaction; instead it had asked the algorithm to focus narrowly on sales. Ultimately, the company's new approach was to become great at forecasting not just how well products would sell but also how much people would enjoy and keep their products. The firm now looks for offerings that customers will rave about on Amazon and other platforms, and the product return rate has plummeted.

This company ran into a common pitfall of dealing with algorithms: Algorithms tend to be myopic. They focus on the data at hand—and that data often pertains to short-term outcomes. There can be a tension between short-term success and long-term profits and broader corporate goals. Humans implicitly understand this; algorithms don't unless you tell them to.

This problem can be solved at the objective-setting phase by identifying and specifying long-term goals. But when acting on an algorithm's predictions, managers should also adjust for the extent to which the algorithm is consistent with long-term aims.

Myopia is also the underlying weakness of programs that produce low-quality content by seeking to maximize click-throughs. The algorithms are optimizing for a goal that can be measured in the moment—whether a user clicks on a link—without regard to the longer-range and more important goal of keeping users satisfied with their experience on the site.

Nearsightedness can similarly be an issue with marketing campaigns. Consider a run-of-the-mill Gap advertising campaign with

Google. It would most likely lead to a spike in visits to Gap.com—because Google's algorithm is good at predicting who will click on an ad. The issue is, the real goal is increasing sales—not increasing website visits. To address this, advertising platforms can collect sales data through a variety of channels, such as partnerships with payment systems, and incorporate it into their algorithms.

What's more, website visits are a short-term behavior, whereas the long-term impact of advertisements includes the downstream effects on brand image and repeat business. While perfect data on such effects is hard to find, careful data audits can help a lot. Managers should systematically list all internal and external data that may be relevant to the project at hand. With a Google campaign, the Gap's marketers could begin by laying out all their objectives—high sales, low returns, good reputation, and so on—and then spell out ways to measure each. Product returns, online reviews, and searches for the term "Gap" would all be great metrics. The best algorithm could then build predictions from a combination of all these features, calibrating for their relative importance.

Choose the Right Data Inputs

Let's return to the example of health departments that are trying to identify restaurants at risk for causing foodborne illness. As mentioned earlier, cities historically have inspected either randomly or on the basis of prior inspection results. Working with Yelp, one of us helped the city of Boston use online reviews to determine which restaurants were most likely to violate local health codes, creating an algorithm that compared the text in reviews with historical inspection data. By applying it, the city identified the same number of violations as usual, but with 40% fewer inspectors—a dramatic increase in efficiency.

This approach worked well not just because we had a lot of restaurants to look at but because Yelp reviews provided a great set of data—something cities hadn't given much thought to. A Yelp review contains many words and a variety of information. The data is also diverse, because it's drawn from different sources. In short, it's quite unlike the inspector-created data cities were accustomed to working with.

When choosing the right data resources, keep in mind the following:

Wider is better

One trap companies often fall into is thinking of big data as simply a lot of records—for example, looking at one million customers instead of 10,000. But this is only half the picture. Imagine your data organized into a table, with a row for each customer. The number of customers is the length of the table. The amount you know about each customer determines the width—how many features are recorded in each row. And while increasing the length of the data will improve your predictions, the full power of big data comes from gathering wide data. Leveraging comprehensive information is at the heart of prediction. Every additional detail you learn about an outcome is like one more clue, and it can be combined with clues you've already collected. Text documents are a great source of wide data, for instance; each word is a clue.

Diversity matters

A corollary to this is that data should be diverse, in the sense that the different data sources should be relatively unrelated to one another. This is where extra predictive power comes from. Treat each data set like a recommendation from a friend. If the data sets are too similar, there won't be much marginal gain from each additional one. But if each data set has a unique perspective, a lot more value is created.

Understand the Limitations

Knowing what your algorithm can't tell you is just as important as knowing what it can. It's easy to succumb to the misguided belief that predictions made in one context will apply equally well in another. That's what prevented the 2009 Netflix competition from yielding more benefit to the company: The algorithm that accurately forecast which DVD a person would want to order in the mail wasn't nearly as good at pinpointing which movie a person would want to stream right now. Netflix got useful insights and good publicity from the contest, but the data it collected on DVDs did not apply to streaming.

Algorithms use existing data to make predictions about what might happen with a slightly different setting, population, time, or question. In essence, you're transferring an insight from one context to another. It's a wise practice, therefore, to list the reasons why the algorithm might not be transferable to a new problem and assess their significance. For instance, a health-code violation algorithm based on reviews and violations in Boston may be less effective in Orlando, which has hotter weather and therefore faces different food safety issues.

Also remember that correlation still doesn't mean causation. Suppose that an algorithm predicts that short tweets will get retweeted more often than longer ones. This does not in any way suggest that you should shorten your tweets. This is a prediction, not advice. It works as a prediction because there are many other factors that correlate with short tweets that make them effective. This is also why it fails as advice: Shortening your tweets will not necessarily change those other factors.

Consider the experiences of eBay, which had been advertising through Google for years. EBay saw that people who viewed those ads were more likely to shop at it than people who did not. What it didn't see was whether the advertisements (which were shown millions of times) were causing people to come to its site. After all, the ads were deliberately shown to likely eBay shoppers. To separate correlation from causation, eBay ran a large experiment in which it randomly advertised to some people and not others. The result? It turns out that the advertisements were for the most part useless, because the people who saw them already knew about eBay and would have shopped there anyway.

———————

Algorithms capable of making predictions do not eliminate the need for care when drawing connections between cause and effect; they are not a replacement for controlled experiments. But what they can do is extremely powerful: identifying patterns too subtle to be detected by human observation, and using those patterns to generate accurate insights and inform better decision making. The challenge for us is to understand their risks and limitations and, through effective management, unlock their remarkable potential.

Originally published in January–February 2016. Reprint R1601H

Pipelines, Platforms, and the New Rules of Strategy

by Marshall W. Van Alstyne, Geoffrey G. Parker, and Sangeet Paul Choudary

BACK IN 2007 the five major mobile-phone manufacturers—Nokia, Samsung, Motorola, Sony Ericsson, and LG—collectively controlled 90% of the industry's global profits. That year, Apple's iPhone burst onto the scene and began gobbling up market share.

By 2015 the iPhone *singlehandedly* generated 92% of global profits, while all but one of the former incumbents made no profit at all.

How can we explain the iPhone's rapid domination of its industry? And how can we explain its competitors' free fall? Nokia and the others had classic strategic advantages that should have protected them: strong product differentiation, trusted brands, leading operating systems, excellent logistics, protective regulation, huge R&D budgets, and massive scale. For the most part, those firms looked stable, profitable, and well entrenched.

Certainly the iPhone had an innovative design and novel capabilities. But in 2007, Apple was a weak, nonthreatening player surrounded by 800-pound gorillas. It had less than 4% of market share in desktop operating systems and none at all in mobile phones.

As we'll explain, Apple (along with Google's competing Android system) overran the incumbents by exploiting the power of platforms and leveraging the new rules of strategy they give rise to. Platform businesses bring together producers and consumers in high-value exchanges. Their chief assets are information and interactions, which together are also the source of the value they create and their competitive advantage.

Understanding this, Apple conceived the iPhone and its operating system as more than a product or a conduit for services. It imagined them as a way to connect participants in two-sided markets—app developers on one side and app users on the other—generating value for both groups. As the number of participants on each side grew, that value increased—a phenomenon called "network effects," which is central to platform strategy. By January 2015 the company's App Store offered 1.4 million apps and had cumulatively generated $25 billion for developers.

Apple's success in building a platform business within a conventional product firm holds critical lessons for companies across industries. Firms that fail to create platforms and don't learn the new rules of strategy will be unable to compete for long.

Pipeline to Platform

Platforms have existed for years. Malls link consumers and merchants; newspapers connect subscribers and advertisers. What's changed in this century is that information technology has profoundly reduced the need to own physical infrastructure and assets. IT makes building and scaling up platforms vastly simpler and cheaper, allows nearly frictionless participation that strengthens network effects, and enhances the ability to capture, analyze, and exchange huge amounts of data that increase the platform's value to all. You don't need to look far to see examples of platform businesses, from Uber to Alibaba to Airbnb, whose spectacular growth abruptly upended their industries.

Though they come in many varieties, platforms all have an ecosystem with the same basic structure, comprising four types of players. The *owners* of platforms control their intellectual property and governance. *Providers* serve as the platforms' interface with users.

Idea in Brief

The Sea Change

Platform businesses that bring together producers and consumers, as Uber and Airbnb do, are gobbling up market share and transforming competition. Traditional businesses that fail to create platforms and to learn the new rules of strategy will struggle.

The New Rules

With a platform, the critical asset is the community and the resources of its members. The focus of strategy shifts from controlling to orchestrating

resources, from optimizing internal processes to facilitating external interactions, and from increasing customer value to maximizing ecosystem value.

The Upshot

In this new world, competition can emerge from seemingly unrelated industries or from within the platform itself. Firms must make smart choices about whom to let onto platforms and what they're allowed to do there, and must track new metrics designed to monitor and boost platform interactions.

Producers create their offerings, and *consumers* use those offerings. (See the exhibit "The players in a platform ecosystem.")

To understand how the rise of platforms is transforming competition, we need to examine how platforms differ from the conventional "pipeline" businesses that have dominated industry for decades. Pipeline businesses create value by controlling a linear series of activities—the classic value-chain model. Inputs at one end of the chain (say, materials from suppliers) undergo a series of steps that transform them into an output that's worth more: the finished product. Apple's handset business is essentially a pipeline. But combine it with the App Store, the marketplace that connects app developers and iPhone owners, and you've got a platform.

As Apple demonstrates, firms needn't be only a pipeline or a platform; they can be both. While plenty of pure pipeline businesses are still highly competitive, when platforms enter the same marketplace, the platforms virtually always win. That's why pipeline giants such as Walmart, Nike, John Deere, and GE are all scrambling to incorporate platforms into their models.

The players in a platform ecosystem

A platform provides the infrastructure and rules for a marketplace that brings together producers and consumers. The players in the ecosystem fill four main roles but may shift rapidly from one role to another. Understanding the relationships both within and outside the ecosystem is central to platform strategy.

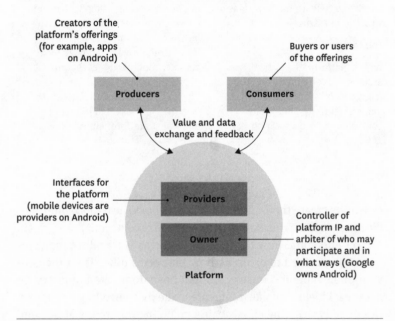

The move from pipeline to platform involves three key shifts:

1. From resource control to resource orchestration. The resource-based view of competition holds that firms gain advantage by controlling scarce and valuable—ideally, inimitable—assets. In a pipeline world, those include tangible assets such as mines and real estate and intangible assets like intellectual property. With platforms, the assets that are hard to copy are the community and the resources its members own and contribute, be they rooms or cars or ideas and information. In other words, the network of producers and consumers is the chief asset.

2. From internal optimization to external interaction. Pipeline firms organize their internal labor and resources to create value by optimizing an entire chain of product activities, from materials sourcing to sales and service. Platforms create value by facilitating interactions between external producers and consumers. Because of this external orientation, they often shed even variable costs of production. The emphasis shifts from dictating processes to persuading participants, and ecosystem governance becomes an essential skill.

3. From a focus on customer value to a focus on ecosystem value. Pipelines seek to maximize the lifetime value of individual customers of products and services, who, in effect, sit at the end of a linear process. By contrast, platforms seek to maximize the total value of an expanding ecosystem in a circular, iterative, feedback-driven process. Sometimes that requires subsidizing one type of consumer in order to attract another type.

These three shifts make clear that competition is more complicated and dynamic in a platform world. The competitive forces described by Michael Porter (the threat of new entrants and substitute products or services, the bargaining power of customers and suppliers, and the intensity of competitive rivalry) still apply. But on platforms these forces behave differently, and new factors come into play. To manage them, executives must pay close attention to the interactions on the platform, participants' access, and new performance metrics.

We'll examine each of these in turn. But first let's look more closely at network effects—the driving force behind every successful platform.

The Power of Network Effects

The engine of the industrial economy was, and remains, supply-side economies of scale. Massive fixed costs and low marginal costs mean that firms achieving higher sales volume than their competitors have a lower average cost of doing business. That allows them to reduce prices, which increases volume further, which permits more price cuts—a virtuous feedback loop that produces monopolies. Supply economics gave us Carnegie Steel, Edison Electric (which became GE), Rockefeller's Standard Oil, and many other industrial era giants.

In supply-side economies, firms achieve market power by controlling resources, ruthlessly increasing efficiency, and fending off challenges from any of the five forces. The goal of strategy in this world is to build a moat around the business that protects it from competition and channels competition toward other firms.

The driving force behind the internet economy, conversely, is demand-side economies of scale, also known as network effects. These are enhanced by technologies that create efficiencies in social networking, demand aggregation, app development, and other phenomena that help networks expand. In the internet economy, firms that achieve higher "volume" than competitors (that is, attract more platform participants) offer a higher average value per transaction. That's because the larger the network, the better the matches between supply and demand and the richer the data that can be used to find matches. Greater scale generates more value, which attracts more participants, which creates more value—another virtuous feedback loop that produces monopolies. Network effects gave us Alibaba, which accounts for over 75% of Chinese e-commerce transactions; Google, which accounts for 82% of mobile operating systems and 94% of mobile search; and Facebook, the world's dominant social platform.

The five forces model doesn't factor in network effects and the value they create. It regards external forces as "depletive," or extracting value from a firm, and so argues for building barriers against them. In demand-side economies, however, external forces can be "accretive"—adding value to the platform business. Thus the power of suppliers and customers, which is threatening in a supply-side world, may be viewed as an asset on platforms. Understanding when external forces may either add or extract value in an ecosystem is central to platform strategy.

How Platforms Change Strategy

In pipeline businesses, the five forces are relatively defined and stable. If you're a cement manufacturer or an airline, your customers and competitive set are fairly well understood, and the boundaries separating your suppliers, customers, and competitors are reasonably clear. In platform businesses, those boundaries can shift rapidly, as we'll discuss.

Forces within the ecosystem

Platform participants—consumers, producers, and providers—typically create value for a business. But they may defect if they believe their needs can be met better elsewhere. More worrisome, they may turn on the platform and compete directly with it. Zynga began as a games producer on Facebook but then sought to migrate players onto its own platform. Amazon and Samsung, providers of devices for the Android platform, tried to create their own versions of the operating system and take consumers with them.

The new roles that players assume can be either accretive or depletive. For example, consumers and producers can swap roles in ways that generate value for the platform. Users can ride with Uber today and drive for it tomorrow; travelers can stay with Airbnb one night and serve as hosts for other customers the next. In contrast, providers on a platform may become depletive, especially if they decide to compete with the owner. Netflix, a provider on the platforms of telecommunication firms, has control of consumers' interactions with the content it offers, so it can extract value from the platform owners while continuing to rely on their infrastructure.

As a consequence, platform firms must constantly encourage accretive activity within their ecosystems while monitoring participants' activity that may prove depletive. This is a delicate governance challenge that we'll discuss further.

Forces exerted by ecosystems

Managers of pipeline businesses can fail to anticipate platform competition from seemingly unrelated industries. Yet successful platform businesses tend to move aggressively into new terrain

Networks Invert the Firm

PIPELINE FIRMS HAVE LONG outsourced aspects of their internal functions, such as customer service. But today companies are taking that shift even further, moving toward orchestrating external networks that can complement or entirely replace the activities of once-internal functions.

Inversion extends outsourcing: Where firms might once have furnished design specifications to a known supplier, they now tap ideas they haven't yet imagined from third parties they don't even know. Firms are being turned inside out as value-creating activities move beyond their direct control and their organizational boundaries.

Marketing is no longer just about creating internally managed outbound messages. It now extends to the creation and propagation of messages by consumers themselves. Travel destination marketers invite consumers to submit videos of their trips and promote them on social media. The online eyeglasses retailer Warby Parker encourages consumers to post online photos of themselves modeling different styles and ask friends to help them choose. Consumers get more-flattering glasses, and Warby Parker gets viral exposure.

Information technology, historically focused on managing internal enterprise systems, increasingly supports external social and community networks. Threadless, a producer of T-shirts, coordinates communication not just to and from but among customers, who collaborate to develop the best product designs.

---

and into what were once considered separate industries with little warning. Google has moved from web search into mapping, mobile operating systems, home automation, driverless cars, and voice recognition. As a result of such shape-shifting, a platform can abruptly transform an incumbent's set of competitors. Swatch knows how to compete with Timex on watches but now must also compete with Apple. Siemens knows how to compete with Honeywell in thermostats but now is being challenged by Google's Nest.

Competitive threats tend to follow one of three patterns. First, they may come from an established platform with superior network effects that uses its relationships with customers to enter your industry. Products have features; platforms have communities, and those communities can be leveraged. Given Google's relation-

Human resources functions at companies increasingly leverage the wisdom of networks to augment internal talent. Enterprise software giant SAP has opened the internal system on which its developers exchange problems and solutions to its external ecosystem—to developers at both its own partners and its partners' clients. Information sharing across this network has improved product development and productivity and reduced support costs.

Finance, which historically has recorded its activities on private internal accounts, now records some transactions externally on public, or "distributed," ledgers. Organizations such as IBM, Intel, and JPMorgan are adopting blockchain technology that allows ledgers to be securely shared and vetted by anyone with permission. Participants can inspect everything from aggregated accounts to individual transactions. This allows firms to, for example, crowdsource compliance with accounting principles or seek input on their financial management from a broad network outside the company. Opening the books this way taps the wisdom of crowds and signals trustworthiness.

Operations and logistics traditionally emphasize the management of just-in-time inventory. More and more often, that function is being supplanted by the management of "not-even-mine" inventory—whether rooms, apps, or other assets owned by network participants. Indeed, if Marriott, Yellow Cab, and NBC had added platforms to their pipeline value chains, then Airbnb, Uber, and YouTube might never have come into being.

---

ship with consumers, the value its network provides them, and its interest in the internet of things, Siemens might have predicted the tech giant's entry into the home-automation market (though not necessarily into thermostats). Second, a competitor may target an overlapping customer base with a distinctive new offering that leverages network effects. Airbnb's and Uber's challenges to the hotel and taxi industries fall into this category. The final pattern, in which platforms that collect the same type of data that your firm does suddenly go after your market, is still emerging. When a data set is valuable, but different parties control different chunks of it, competition between unlikely camps may ensue. This is happening in health care, where traditional providers, producers of wearables like Fitbit, and retail pharmacies like Walgreens are all launching platforms based on the health data they own. They can be expected to compete for control of a broader data set—and the consumer relationships that come with it.

Focus

Managers of pipeline businesses focus on growing sales. For them, goods and services delivered (and the revenues and profits from them) are the units of analysis. For platforms, the focus shifts to interactions—exchanges of value between producers and consumers on the platform. The unit of exchange (say, a view of a video or a thumbs-up on a post) can be so small that little or no money changes hands. Nevertheless, the number of interactions and the associated network effects are the ultimate source of competitive advantage.

With platforms, a critical strategic aim is strong up-front design that will attract the desired participants, enable the right interactions (so-called core interactions), and encourage ever-more-powerful network effects. In our experience, managers often fumble here by focusing too much on the wrong type of interaction. And the perhaps counterintuitive bottom line, given how much we stress the importance of network effects, is that it's usually wise to ensure the value of interactions for participants before focusing on volume.

Most successful platforms launch with a single type of interaction that generates high value even if, at first, low volume. They then move into adjacent markets or adjacent types of interactions, increasing both value and volume. Facebook, for example, launched with a narrow focus (connecting Harvard students to other Harvard students) and then opened the platform to college students broadly and ultimately to everyone. LinkedIn launched as a professional networking site and later entered new markets with recruitment, publishing, and other offerings.

Access and governance

In a pipeline world, strategy revolves around erecting barriers. With platforms, while guarding against threats remains critical, the focus of strategy shifts to eliminating barriers to production and consumption in order to maximize value creation. To that end,

Harnessing Spillovers

POSITIVE SPILLOVER EFFECTS help platforms rapidly increase the volume of interactions. Book purchases on a platform, for example, generate book recommendations that create value for other participants on it, who then buy more books. This dynamic exploits the fact that network effects are often strongest among interactions of the same type (say, book sales) than among unrelated interactions (say, package pickup and yardwork in different cities mediated by the odd-job platform TaskRabbit).

Consider ride sharing. By itself, an individual ride on Uber is high value for both rider and driver—a desirable core interaction. As the number of platform participants increases, so does the value Uber delivers to both sides of the market; it becomes easier for consumers to get rides and for drivers to find fares. Spillover effects further enhance the value of Uber to participants: Data from riders' interactions with drivers—ratings of drivers and riders—improves the value of the platform to other users. Similarly, data on how well a given ride matched a rider's needs helps determine optimal pricing across the platform—another important spillover effect.

platform executives must make smart choices about access (whom to let onto the platform) and governance (or "control"—what consumers, producers, providers, and even competitors are allowed to do there).

Platforms consist of rules and architecture. Their owners need to decide how open both should be. An *open architecture* allows players to access platform resources, such as app developer tools, and create new sources of value. *Open governance* allows players other than the owner to shape the rules of trade and reward sharing on the platform. Regardless of who sets the rules, a fair reward system is key. If managers open the architecture but do not share the rewards, potential platform participants (such as app developers) have the ability to engage but no incentives. If managers open the rules and rewards but keep the architecture relatively closed, potential participants have incentives to engage but not the ability.

These choices aren't fixed. Platforms often launch with a fairly closed architecture and governance and then open up as they introduce new types of interactions and sources of value. But every platform must induce producers and consumers to interact and share their ideas and resources. Effective governance will inspire outsiders to bring valuable intellectual property to the platform, as Zynga did in bringing FarmVille to Facebook. That won't happen if prospective partners fear exploitation.

Some platforms encourage producers to create high-value offerings on them by establishing a policy of "permissionless innovation." They let producers invent things for the platform without approval but guarantee the producers will share in the value created. Rovio, for example, didn't need permission to create the Angry Birds game on the Apple operating system and could be confident that Apple wouldn't steal its IP. The result was a hit that generated enormous value for all participants on the platform. However, Google's Android platform has allowed even more innovation to flourish by being more open at the provider layer. That decision is one reason Google's market capitalization surpassed Apple's in early 2016 (just as Microsoft's did in the 1980s).

However, unfettered access can destroy value by creating "noise"—misbehavior or excess or low-quality content that inhibits interaction. One company that ran into this problem was Chatroulette, which paired random people from around the world for webchats. It grew exponentially until noise caused its abrupt collapse. Initially utterly open—it had no access rules at all—it soon encountered the "naked hairy man" problem, which is exactly what it sounds like. Clothed users abandoned the platform in droves. Chatroulette responded by reducing its openness with a variety of user filters.

Most successful platforms similarly manage openness to maximize positive network effects. Airbnb and Uber rate and insure hosts and drivers, Twitter and Facebook provide users with tools to prevent stalking, and Apple's App Store and the Google Play store both filter out low-quality applications.

Metrics

Leaders of pipeline enterprises have long focused on a narrow set of metrics that capture the health of their businesses. For example, pipelines grow by optimizing processes and opening bottlenecks;

one standard metric, inventory turnover, tracks the flow of goods and services through them. Push enough goods through and get margins high enough, and you'll see a reasonable rate of return.

As pipelines launch platforms, however, the numbers to watch change. Monitoring and boosting the performance of core interactions becomes critical. Here are new metrics managers need to track:

Interaction failure. If a traveler opens the Lyft app and sees "no cars available," the platform has failed to match an intent to consume with supply. Failures like these directly diminish network effects. Passengers who see this message too often will stop using Lyft, leading to higher driver downtimes, which can cause drivers to quit Lyft, resulting in even lower ride availability. Feedback loops can strengthen or weaken a platform.

Engagement. Healthy platforms track the participation of ecosystem members that enhances network effects—activities such as content sharing and repeat visits. Facebook, for example, watches the ratio of daily to monthly users to gauge the effectiveness of its efforts to increase engagement.

Match quality. Poor matches between the needs of users and producers weaken network effects. Google constantly monitors users' clicking and reading to refine how its search results fill their requests.

Negative network effects. Badly managed platforms often suffer from other kinds of problems that create negative feedback loops and reduce value. For example, congestion caused by unconstrained network growth can discourage participation. So can misbehavior, as Chatroulette found. Managers must watch for negative network effects and use governance tools to stem them by, for example, withholding privileges or banishing troublemakers.

Finally, platforms must understand the financial value of their communities and their network effects. Consider that in 2016, private equity markets placed the value of Uber, a demand economy firm founded in 2009, above that of GM, a supply economy firm founded in 1908. Clearly Uber's investors were looking beyond the traditional financials and metrics when calculating the firm's worth and potential. This is a clear indication that the rules have changed.

Because platforms require new approaches to strategy, they also demand new leadership styles. The skills it takes to tightly control internal resources just don't apply to the job of nurturing external ecosystems.

While pure platforms naturally launch with an external orientation, traditional pipeline firms must develop new core competencies—and a new mindset—to design, govern, and nimbly expand platforms on top of their existing businesses. The inability to make this leap explains why some traditional business leaders with impressive track records falter in platforms. Media mogul Rupert Murdoch bought the social network Myspace and managed it the way he might have run a newspaper—from the top down, bureaucratically, and with a focus more on controlling the internal operation than on fostering the ecosystem and creating value for participants. In time the Myspace community dissipated and the platform withered.

The failure to transition to a new approach explains the precarious situation that traditional businesses—from hotels to health care providers to taxis—find themselves in. For pipeline firms, the writing is on the wall: Learn the new rules of strategy for a platform world, or begin planning your exit.

Originally published in April 2016. Reprint R1604C

What Is Disruptive Innovation?

by Clayton M. Christensen, Michael Raynor, and Rory McDonald

THE THEORY OF DISRUPTIVE INNOVATION, introduced in these pages in 1995, has proved to be a powerful way of thinking about innovation-driven growth. Many leaders of small, entrepreneurial companies praise it as their guiding star; so do many executives at large, well-established organizations, including Intel, Southern New Hampshire University, and Salesforce.com.

Unfortunately, disruption theory is in danger of becoming a victim of its own success. Despite broad dissemination, the theory's core concepts have been widely misunderstood and its basic tenets frequently misapplied. Furthermore, essential refinements in the theory over the past 20 years appear to have been overshadowed by the popularity of the initial formulation. As a result, the theory is sometimes criticized for shortcomings that have already been addressed.

There's another troubling concern: In our experience, too many people who speak of "disruption" have not read a serious book or article on the subject. Too frequently, they use the term loosely to invoke the concept of innovation in support of whatever it is they wish to do. Many researchers, writers, and consultants use "disruptive innovation" to describe *any* situation in which an industry is shaken up and previously successful incumbents stumble. But that's much too broad a usage.

The problem with conflating a disruptive innovation with any breakthrough that changes an industry's competitive patterns is that different types of innovation require different strategic approaches. To put it another way, the lessons we've learned about succeeding as a disruptive innovator (or defending against a disruptive challenger) will not apply to every company in a shifting market. If we get sloppy with our labels or fail to integrate insights from subsequent research and experience into the original theory, then managers may end up using the wrong tools for their context, reducing their chances of success. Over time, the theory's usefulness will be undermined.

This article is part of an effort to capture the state of the art. We begin by exploring the basic tenets of disruptive innovation and examining whether they apply to Uber. Then we point out some common pitfalls in the theory's application, how these arise, and why correctly using the theory matters. We go on to trace major turning points in the evolution of our thinking and make the case that what we have learned allows us to more accurately predict which businesses will grow.

First, a quick recap of the idea: "Disruption" describes a process whereby a smaller company with fewer resources is able to successfully challenge established incumbent businesses. Specifically, as incumbents focus on improving their products and services for their most demanding (and usually most profitable) customers, they exceed the needs of some segments and ignore the needs of others. Entrants that prove disruptive begin by successfully targeting those overlooked segments, gaining a foothold by delivering more-suitable functionality—frequently at a lower price. Incumbents, chasing higher profitability in more-demanding segments, tend not to respond vigorously. Entrants then move upmarket, delivering the performance that incumbents' mainstream customers require, while preserving the advantages that drove their early success. When mainstream customers start adopting the entrants' offerings in volume, disruption has occurred. (See the exhibit "The disruptive innovation model.")

Idea in Brief

The Issue

The ideas summed up in the phrase "disruptive innovation" have become a powerful part of business thinking—but they're in danger of losing their usefulness because they've been misunderstood and misapplied.

The Response

The leading authorities on disruptive innovation revisit the central tenets of disruption theory, its development over the past 20 years, and its limitations.

The Bottom Line

Does it matter whether Uber, say, is a disruptive innovation or something else entirely? It does: We can't manage innovation effectively if we don't grasp its true nature.

Is Uber a Disruptive Innovation?

Let's consider Uber, the much-feted transportation company whose mobile application connects consumers who need rides with drivers who are willing to provide them. Founded in 2009, the company has enjoyed fantastic growth (it operates in hundreds of cities in 60 countries and is still expanding). It has reported tremendous financial success (the most recent funding round implies an enterprise value in the vicinity of $50 billion). And it has spawned a slew of imitators (other start-ups are trying to emulate its "market-making" business model). Uber is clearly transforming the taxi business in the United States. But is it *disrupting* the taxi business?

According to the theory, the answer is no. Uber's financial and strategic achievements do not qualify the company as genuinely disruptive—although the company is almost always described that way. Here are two reasons why the label doesn't fit.

Disruptive innovations originate in low-end or new-market footholds

Disruptive innovations are made possible because they get started in two types of markets that incumbents overlook. *Low-end footholds* exist because incumbents typically try to provide their most

The disruptive innovation model

This diagram contrasts product performance trajectories *(the dashed lines showing how products or services improve over time)* with customer demand trajectories *(the solid lines showing customers' willingness to pay for performance). As incumbent companies introduce higher-quality products or services (upper dashed line) to satisfy the high end of the market (where profitability is highest), they overshoot the needs of low-end customers and many mainstream customers. This leaves an opening for entrants to find footholds in the less-profitable segments that incumbents are neglecting. Entrants on a disruptive trajectory (lower dashed line) improve the performance of their offerings and move upmarket (where profitability is highest for them, too) and challenge the dominance of the incumbents.*

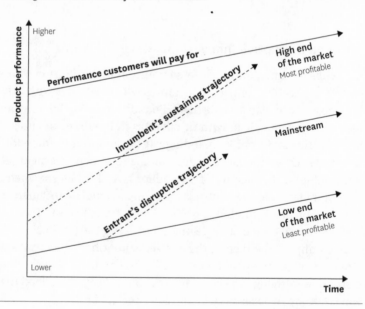

profitable and demanding customers with ever-improving products and services, and they pay less attention to less-demanding customers. In fact, incumbents' offerings often overshoot the performance requirements of the latter. This opens the door to a disrupter focused (at first) on providing those low-end customers with a "good enough" product.

In the case of *new-market footholds,* disrupters create a market where none existed. Put simply, they find a way to turn nonconsumers into consumers. For example, in the early days of photocopying technology, Xerox targeted large corporations and charged high prices in order to provide the performance that those customers required. School librarians, bowling-league operators, and other small customers, priced out of the market, made do with carbon paper or mimeograph machines. Then in the late 1970s, new challengers introduced personal copiers, offering an affordable solution to individuals and small organizations—and a new market was created. From this relatively modest beginning, personal photocopier makers gradually built a major position in the mainstream photocopier market that Xerox valued.

A disruptive innovation, by definition, starts from one of those two footholds. But Uber did not originate in either one. It is difficult to claim that the company found a low-end opportunity: That would have meant taxi service providers had overshot the needs of a material number of customers by making cabs too plentiful, too easy to use, and too clean. Neither did Uber primarily target nonconsumers—people who found the existing alternatives so expensive or inconvenient that they took public transit or drove themselves instead: Uber was launched in San Francisco (a well-served taxi market), and Uber's customers were generally people already in the habit of hiring rides.

Uber has quite arguably been increasing total demand—that's what happens when you develop a better, less-expensive solution to a widespread customer need. But disrupters *start* by appealing to low-end or unserved consumers and then migrate to the mainstream market. Uber has gone in exactly the opposite direction: building a position in the mainstream market first and subsequently appealing to historically overlooked segments.

Disruptive innovations don't catch on with mainstream customers until quality catches up to their standards

Disruption theory differentiates disruptive innovations from what are called "sustaining innovations." The latter make good products better in the eyes of an incumbent's existing customers: the fifth blade in a razor, the clearer TV picture, better mobile phone reception. These improvements can be incremental advances or major breakthroughs, but they all enable firms to sell more products to their most profitable customers.

Disruptive innovations, on the other hand, are initially considered inferior by most of an incumbent's customers. Typically, customers are not willing to switch to the new offering merely because it is less expensive. Instead, they wait until its quality rises enough to satisfy them. Once that's happened, they adopt the new product and happily accept its lower price. (This is how disruption drives prices down in a market.)

Most of the elements of Uber's strategy seem to be sustaining innovations. Uber's service has rarely been described as inferior to existing taxis; in fact, many would say it is *better*. Booking a ride requires just a few taps on a smartphone; payment is cashless and convenient; and passengers can rate their rides afterward, which helps ensure high standards. Furthermore, Uber delivers service reliably and punctually, and its pricing is usually competitive with (or lower than) that of established taxi services. And as is typical when incumbents face threats from sustaining innovations, many of the taxi companies are motivated to respond. They are deploying competitive technologies, such as hailing apps, and contesting the legality of some of Uber's services.

Why Getting It Right Matters

Readers may still be wondering, Why does it matter what words we use to describe Uber? The company has certainly thrown the taxi industry into disarray: Isn't that "disruptive" enough? No. Applying the theory correctly is essential to realizing its benefits. For example, small competitors that nibble away at the periphery of your business very likely should be ignored—unless they are on a disruptive trajectory, in which case they are a potentially mortal threat. And both of these challenges are fundamentally different from efforts by competitors to woo your bread-and-butter customers.

As the example of Uber shows, identifying true disruptive inno-vation is tricky. Yet even executives with a good understanding of disruption theory tend to forget some of its subtler aspects when making strategic decisions. We've observed four important points that get overlooked or misunderstood:

1. Disruption is a process

The term "disruptive innovation" is misleading when it is used to refer to a product or service at one fixed point, rather than to the evolution of that product or service over time. The first minicom-puters were disruptive not merely because they were low-end up-starts when they appeared on the scene, nor because they were later heralded as superior to mainframes in many markets; they were dis-ruptive by virtue of the path they followed from the fringe to the mainstream.

Most every innovation—disruptive or not—begins life as a small-scale experiment. Disrupters tend to focus on getting the business model, rather than merely the product, just right. When they succeed, their movement from the fringe (the low end of the market or a new market) to the mainstream erodes first the incumbents' market share and then their profitability. This process can take time, and incumbents can get quite creative in the defense of their established franchises. For example, more than 50 years after the first discount department store was opened, mainstream retail companies still operate their traditional department-store formats. Complete substitution, if it comes at all, may take decades, because the incremental profit from staying with the old model for one more year trumps proposals to write off the assets in one stroke.

The fact that disruption can take time helps to explain why in-cumbents frequently overlook disrupters. For example, when Net-flix launched, in 1997, its initial service wasn't appealing to most of Blockbuster's customers, who rented movies (typically new re-leases) on impulse. Netflix had an exclusively online interface and a large inventory of movies, but delivery through the U.S. mail meant selections took several days to arrive. The service appealed to only a few customer groups—movie buffs who didn't care about new releases, early adopters of DVD players, and online shoppers. If Netflix had not eventually begun to serve a broader segment of the market, Blockbuster's decision to ignore this competitor would not have been a strategic blunder: The two companies filled very different needs for their (different) customers.

However, as new technologies allowed Netflix to shift to streaming video over the internet, the company did eventually become appealing to Blockbuster's core customers, offering a wider selection of content with an all-you-can-watch, on-demand, low-price, high-quality, highly convenient approach. And it got there via a classically disruptive path. If Netflix (like Uber) had begun by launching a service targeted at a larger competitor's core market, Blockbuster's response would very likely have been a vigorous and perhaps successful counterattack. But failing to respond effectively to the trajectory that Netflix was on led Blockbuster to collapse.

2. Disrupters often build business models that are very different from those of incumbents

Consider the health care industry. General practitioners operating out of their offices often rely on their years of experience and on test results to interpret patients' symptoms, make diagnoses, and prescribe treatment. We call this a "solution shop" business model. In contrast, a number of convenient care clinics are taking a disruptive path by using what we call a "process" business model: They follow standardized protocols to diagnose and treat a small but increasing number of disorders.

One high-profile example of using an innovative business model to effect a disruption is Apple's iPhone. The product that Apple debuted in 2007 was a sustaining innovation in the smartphone market: It targeted the same customers coveted by incumbents, and its initial success is likely explained by product superiority. The iPhone's subsequent growth is better explained by disruption—not of other smartphones but of the laptop as the primary access point to the internet. This was achieved not merely through product improvements but also through the introduction of a new business model. By building a facilitated network connecting application developers with phone users, Apple changed the game. The iPhone created a new market for internet access and eventually was able to challenge laptops as mainstream users' device of choice for going online.

3. Some disruptive innovations succeed; some don't

A third common mistake is to focus on the results achieved—to claim that a company is disruptive by virtue of its success. But success is not built into the definition of disruption: Not every disruptive path leads to a triumph, and not every triumphant newcomer follows a disruptive path.

For example, any number of internet-based retailers pursued disruptive paths in the late 1990s, but only a small number prospered. The failures are not evidence of the deficiencies of disruption theory; they are simply boundary markers for the theory's application. The theory says very little about how to win in the foothold market, other than to play the odds and avoid head-on competition with better-resourced incumbents.

If we call every business success a "disruption," then companies that rise to the top in very different ways will be seen as sources of insight into a common strategy for succeeding. This creates a danger: Managers may mix and match behaviors that are very likely inconsistent with one another and thus unlikely to yield the hoped-for result. For example, both Uber and Apple's iPhone owe their success to a platform-based model: Uber digitally connects riders with drivers; the iPhone connects app developers with phone users. But Uber, true to its nature as a sustaining innovation, has focused on expanding its network and functionality in ways that make it better than traditional taxis. Apple, on the other hand, has followed a disruptive path by building its ecosystem of app developers so as to make the iPhone more like a personal computer.

4. The mantra "Disrupt or be disrupted" can misguide us

Incumbent companies do need to respond to disruption if it's occurring, but they should not overreact by dismantling a still-profitable business. Instead, they should continue to strengthen relationships with core customers by investing in sustaining innovations.

In addition, they can create a new division focused solely on the growth opportunities that arise from the disruption. Our research suggests that the success of this new enterprise depends in large part on keeping it separate from the core business. That means that for some time, incumbents will find themselves managing two very different operations.

Of course, as the disruptive stand-alone business grows, it may eventually steal customers from the core. But corporate leaders should not try to solve this problem before it *is* a problem.

What a Disruptive Innovation Lens Can Reveal

It is rare that a technology or product is inherently sustaining or disruptive. And when new technology is developed, disruption theory does not dictate what managers should do. Instead it helps them make a strategic choice between taking a sustaining path and taking a disruptive one.

The theory of disruption predicts that when an entrant tackles incumbent competitors head-on, offering better products or services, the incumbents will accelerate their innovations to defend their business. Either they will beat back the entrant by offering even better services or products at comparable prices, or one of them will acquire the entrant. The data supports the theory's prediction that entrants pursuing a sustaining strategy for a stand-alone business will face steep odds: In Christensen's seminal study of the disk drive industry, only 6% of sustaining entrants managed to succeed.

Uber's strong performance therefore warrants explanation. According to disruption theory, Uber is an outlier, and we do not have a universal way to account for such atypical outcomes. In Uber's case, we believe that the regulated nature of the taxi business is a large part of the answer. Market entry and prices are closely controlled in many jurisdictions. Consequently, taxi companies have rarely innovated. Individual drivers have few ways to innovate, except to defect to Uber. So Uber is in a unique situation relative to taxis: It can offer better quality and the competition will find it hard to respond, at least in the short term.

The ubiquitous "disruptive innovation"

"Disruptive innovation" and "disruptive technology" are now part of the popular business lexicon, as suggested by the dramatic growth in the number of articles using those phrases in recent years.

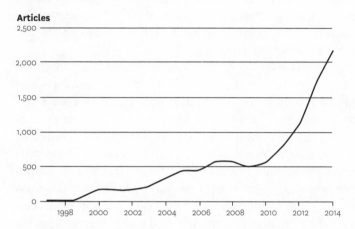

Articles

Source: Factiva analysis of a wide variety of English-language publications

To this point, we've addressed only whether or not Uber is disruptive to the taxi business. The limousine or "black car" business is a different story, and here Uber is far more likely to be on a disruptive path. The company's UberSELECT option provides more-luxurious cars and is typically more expensive than its standard service—but typically less expensive than hiring a traditional limousine. This lower price imposes some compromises, as UberSELECT currently does not include one defining feature of the leading incumbents in this market: acceptance of advance reservations. Consequently, this offering from Uber appeals to the low end of the limousine service market: customers willing to sacrifice a measure of convenience for monetary savings. Should Uber find ways to match or exceed incumbents' performance levels without compromising its cost and price advantage, the company appears to be well positioned to move into the mainstream of the limo business—and it will have done so in classically disruptive fashion.

How Our Thinking About Disruption Has Developed

Initially, the theory of disruptive innovation was simply a statement about correlation. Empirical findings showed that incumbents outperformed entrants in a sustaining innovation context but underperformed in a disruptive innovation context. The reason for this correlation was not immediately evident, but one by one, the elements of the theory fell into place.

First, researchers realized that a company's propensity for strategic change is profoundly affected by the interests of customers who provide the resources the firm needs to survive. In other words, incumbents (sensibly) listen to their existing customers and concentrate on sustaining innovations as a result. Researchers then arrived at a second insight: Incumbents' focus on their existing customers becomes institutionalized in internal processes that make it difficult for even senior managers to shift investment to disruptive innovations. For example, interviews with managers of established companies in the disk drive industry revealed that resource allocation processes prioritized sustaining innovations (which had high margins and targeted large markets with well-known customers) while inadvertently starving disruptive innovations (meant for smaller markets with poorly defined customers).

Those two insights helped explain why incumbents rarely responded effectively (if at all) to disruptive innovations, but not why entrants eventually moved upmarket to challenge incumbents, over and over again. It turns out, however, that the same forces leading incumbents to ignore early-stage disruptions also compel disrupters ultimately to disrupt.

What we've realized is that, very often, low-end and new-market footholds are populated not by a lone would-be disrupter, but by several comparable entrant firms whose products are simpler, more convenient, or less costly than those sold by incumbents. The incumbents provide a de facto price umbrella, allowing many of the entrants to enjoy profitable growth within the foothold market. But that lasts only for a time: As incumbents (rationally, but mistakenly) cede the foothold market, they effectively remove the price umbrella, and price-based competition among the entrants reigns. Some entrants will founder, but the smart ones—the true disrupters—will improve their products and drive upmarket, where, once again, they can compete at the margin against higher-cost established competitors. The disruptive effect drives every competitor—incumbent and entrant—upmarket.

With those explanations in hand, the theory of disruptive innovation went beyond simple correlation to a theory of causation as well. The key elements of that theory have been tested and validated through studies of many industries, including retail, computers, printing, motorcycles, cars, semiconductors, cardiovascular surgery, management education, financial services, management consulting, cameras, communications, and computer-aided design software.

Making sense of anomalies

Additional refinements to the theory have been made to address certain anomalies, or unexpected scenarios, that the theory could not explain. For example, we originally assumed that any disruptive innovation took root in the lowest tiers of an established market—yet sometimes new entrants seemed to be competing in entirely new markets. This led to the distinction we discussed earlier between low-end and new-market footholds.

Low-end disrupters (think steel minimills and discount retailers) come in at the bottom of the market and take hold within an existing value network before moving upmarket and attacking that stratum (think integrated steel mills and traditional retailers). By contrast, new-market disruptions take hold in a completely new value network and appeal to customers who have previously gone without the product. Consider the transistor pocket radio and the PC: They were largely ignored by manufacturers of tabletop radios and minicomputers, respectively, because they were aimed at nonconsumers of those goods. By postulating that there are two flavors of foothold markets in which disruptive innovation can begin, the theory has become more powerful and practicable.

Another intriguing anomaly was the identification of industries that have resisted the forces of disruption, at least until very recently. Higher education in the United States is one of these. Over the years—indeed, over more than 100 years—new kinds of institutions with different initial charters have been created to address the needs of various population segments, including nonconsumers. Land-grant universities, teachers' colleges, two-year colleges, and so on were initially launched to serve those for whom a traditional four-year liberal arts education was out of reach or unnecessary.

Many of these new entrants strived to improve over time, compelled by analogues of the pursuit of profitability: a desire for growth, prestige, and the capacity to do greater good. Thus they made costly investments in research, dormitories, athletic facilities, faculty, and so on, seeking to emulate more-elite institutions. Doing so has increased their level of performance in some ways—they can provide richer learning and living environments for students, for example. Yet the *relative* standing of higher-education institutions remains largely unchanged: With few exceptions, the top 20 are still the top 20, and the next 50 are still in that second tier, decade after decade.

Because both incumbents and newcomers are seemingly following the same game plan, it is perhaps no surprise that incumbents are able to maintain their positions. What has been missing—until recently—is experimentation with new models that successfully appeal to today's nonconsumers of higher education.

The question now is whether there is a novel technology or business model that allows new entrants to move upmarket without emulating the incumbents' high costs—that is, to follow a disruptive path. The answer seems to be yes, and the enabling innovation is online learning, which is becoming broadly available. Real tuition for online courses is falling, and accessibility and quality are improving. Innovators are making inroads into the mainstream market at a stunning pace.

Will online education disrupt the incumbents' model? And if so, when? In other words, will online education's trajectory of improvement intersect with the needs of the mainstream market? We've come to realize that the steepness of any disruptive trajectory is a function of how quickly the enabling technology improves. In the steel industry, continuous-casting technology improved quite slowly, and it took more than 40 years before the minimill Nucor matched the revenue of the largest integrated steelmakers. In contrast, the digital technologies that allowed personal computers to disrupt minicomputers improved much more quickly; Compaq was able to increase revenue more than tenfold and reach parity with the industry leader, DEC, in only 12 years.

Understanding what drives the rate of disruption is helpful for predicting outcomes, but it doesn't alter the way disruptions should be managed. Rapid disruptions are not fundamentally different from any others; they don't have different causal mechanisms and don't require conceptually different responses.

Similarly, it is a mistake to assume that the strategies adopted by some high-profile entrants constitute a special kind of disruption. Often these are simply miscategorized. Tesla Motors is a current and salient example. One might be tempted to say the company is disruptive. But its foothold is in the high end of the auto market (with customers willing to spend $70,000 or more on a car), and this segment is not uninteresting to incumbents. Tesla's entry, not surprisingly, has elicited significant attention and investment from established competitors. If disruption theory is correct, Tesla's future holds either acquisition by a much larger incumbent or a years-long and hard-fought battle for market significance.

We still have a lot to learn
We are eager to keep expanding and refining the theory of disruptive innovation, and much work lies ahead. For example, universally effective responses to disruptive threats remain elusive. Our current belief is that companies should create a separate division that operates under the protection of senior leadership to explore and exploit a new disruptive model. Sometimes this works—and sometimes it doesn't. In certain cases, a failed response to a disruptive threat cannot be attributed to a lack of understanding, insufficient executive attention, or inadequate financial investment. The challenges that

arise from being an incumbent and an entrant simultaneously have yet to be fully specified; how best to meet those challenges is still to be discovered.

Disruption theory does not, and never will, explain everything about innovation specifically or business success generally. Far too many other forces are in play, each of which will reward further study. Integrating them all into a comprehensive theory of business success is an ambitious goal, one we are unlikely to attain anytime soon.

But there is cause for hope: Empirical tests show that using disruptive theory makes us measurably and significantly more accurate in our predictions of which fledgling businesses will succeed. As an ever-growing community of researchers and practitioners continues to build on disruption theory and integrate it with other perspectives, we will come to an even better understanding of what helps firms innovate successfully.

Originally published in December 2015. Reprint R1512B

How Indra Nooyi Turned Design Thinking into Strategy

An interview with Indra Nooyi by Adi Ignatius

JUST A FEW YEARS AGO, it wasn't clear whether Indra Nooyi would survive as PepsiCo's CEO. Many investors saw Pepsi as a bloated giant whose top brands were losing market share. And they were critical of Nooyi's shift toward a more health-oriented overall product line. Prominent activist investor Nelson Peltz fought hard to split the company in two.

These days Nooyi, 59, exudes confidence. The company has enjoyed steady revenue growth during her nine years in the top job, and Pepsi's stock price is rising again after several flat years. Peltz even agreed to a truce in return for a board seat for one of his allies.

All of this frees Nooyi to focus on what she says is now driving innovation in the company: design thinking. In 2012 she brought in Mauro Porcini as Pepsi's first-ever chief design officer. Now, Nooyi says, "design" has a voice in nearly every important decision that the company makes. (See the sidebar "How Design Can Thrive.")

To understand Pepsi's transformation, I spoke with Nooyi at the company's temporary headquarters in White Plains, New York (the real one, in Purchase, is being renovated). She talked about what design means to her, the challenges in changing a culture, and her proudest achievement.

—*Adi Ignatius*

HBR: *What problem were you trying to solve by making PepsiCo more design-driven?*

Nooyi: As CEO, I visit a market every week to see what we look like on the shelves. I always ask myself—not as a CEO but as a mom—"What products really speak to me?" The shelves just seem more and more cluttered, so I thought we had to rethink our innovation process and design experiences for our consumers—from conception to what's on the shelf.

How did you begin to drive that change?

First, I gave each of my direct reports an empty photo album and a camera. I asked them to take pictures of anything they thought represented good design.

What did you get back from them?

After six weeks, only a few people returned the albums. Some had their wives take pictures. Many did nothing at all. They didn't know what design was. Every time I tried to talk about design within the company, people would refer to packaging: "Should we go to a different blue?" It was like putting lipstick on a pig, as opposed to redesigning the pig itself. I realized we needed to bring a designer into the company.

How easy was it to find Mauro Porcini?

We did a search, and we saw that he'd achieved this kind of success at 3M. So we brought him in to talk about our vision. He said he wanted resources, a design studio, and a seat at the table. We gave him all of that. Now our teams are pushing design through the entire system, from product creation, to packaging and labeling, to how a product looks on the shelf, to how consumers interact with it.

How Design Can Thrive

MAURO PORCINI, PepsiCo's first-ever chief design officer, oversees design-led innovation across all of PepsiCo's brands. He describes a step-by-step approach to embedding design thinking in a company's culture.

Certain circumstances are necessary for design to thrive in enterprises. First, you have to bring in the right kind of design leaders. That's where many organizations make mistakes. If design is really about deeply understanding people and then strategizing accordingly, we need design leaders with broad skills. Corporate executives often don't understand that there are different kinds of design: brand design, industrial design, interior design, UX (user experience) design, design innovation, and more. So, you need a leader with a holistic vision who can manage all aspects of design in a very smart way.

Second, you need the right sponsorship from the top. The new design function and the new culture must be protected by the CEO or by somebody else at the executive level—because any entity, any organization, is apt to resist change.

Third, with leadership and C-suite sponsorship in place, you need as many external endorsements as possible—from a variety of entities. They might come from business leaders or designers outside your organization, from design and business magazines, or from awards you win. Whatever the sources, those endorsements validate the vision of the people inside your organization, showing them that they're moving in the right direction and building their confidence to proceed.

Then you need quick wins: projects that rapidly prove the value of design inside the enterprise. On the basis of that early success, you start to build a design organization, to create processes that facilitate the new culture, and to craft an approach that can be integrated throughout the whole company.

What's your definition of good design?

For me, a well-designed product is one you fall in love with. Or you hate. It may be polarizing, but it has to provoke a real reaction. Ideally, it's a product you want to engage with in the future, rather than just "Yeah, I bought it, and I ate it."

You say it's not just about packaging, but a lot of what you're talking about seems to be that.

It's much more than packaging. We had to rethink the entire experience, from conception to what's on the shelf to the postproduct experience. Let's take Pepsi Spire, our new touchscreen fountain machine. Other companies with dispensing machines have focused on adding a few more buttons and combinations of flavors. Our design guys essentially said that we're talking about a fundamentally different interaction between consumer and machine. We basically have a gigantic iPad on a futuristic machine that talks to you and invites you to interact with it. It tracks what you buy so that in the future, when you swipe your ID, it reminds you of the flavor combinations you tried last time and suggests new ones. It displays beautiful shots of the product, so when you add lime or cranberry, it actually shows those flavors being added—you *experience* the infusion of the flavor, as opposed to merely hitting a button and out comes the finished product.

Have you developed other notable design-led innovations?

We're working on new products for women. Our old approach was "shrink it or pink it." We'd put Doritos, say, in a pink Susan G. Komen bag and say it's for women. That's fine, but there's more to how women like to snack.

OK, how do women like to snack?

When men finish a snack bag, they pour what's left into their mouths. Women don't do that. And they worry about how much the product may stain—they won't rub it on a chair, which a lot of guys do. In China, we've introduced a stacked chip that comes in a plastic tray inside a canister. When a woman wants to snack, she can open her drawer and eat from the tray. When she's done, she can push it back in. The chip is also less noisy to eat: Women don't want people to hear them crunching away.

Basically, you're paying a lot more attention to user experience.

Definitely. In the past, user experience wasn't part of our lexicon. Focusing on crunch, taste, and everything else now pushes us to rethink shape, packaging, form, and function. All of that has consequences for what machinery we put in place—to produce, say, a plastic tray instead of a flex bag. We're forcing the design thinking way back in the supply chain.

To what extent do you listen to consumers? Do they even know what they want?

I don't know if consumers know what they want. But we can learn from them. Let's take SunChips. The original size was one inch by one inch. When you'd bite into a chip, it would break into pieces. In focus groups consumers told us they went to another product because it was bite-size. We had to conclude that SunChips were too damn big. I don't care if our mold can only cut one inch by one inch. We don't sell products based on the manufacturing we have, but on how our target consumers can fall in love with them.

Launch and Failure

When I picture design thinking, I think about rapid prototyping and testing. Is that part of what you're trying to do?

Not so much in the U.S., but China and Japan are lead horses for that process—test, prove, launch. If you launch quickly, you have more failures, but that's OK because the cost of failure in those markets is low. In the U.S., we tend to follow very organized processes and then launch. The China-Japan model may have to come to the U.S. at some point.

Isn't this model already established in the U.S., or at least in Silicon Valley?

Lots of small companies take this approach, and for them the cost of failure is acceptable. We're more cautious, especially when playing with big brands. Line extensions are fine: If you launch a flavor of Doritos that doesn't work, you just pull it. But if you launch a new product, you want to make sure you've tested it enough. In Japan, we launch a new version of Pepsi every three months—green, pink, blue. We just launched cucumber-flavored Pepsi. In three months it either works or we pull it and go to the next product.

Is your design approach giving Pepsi competitive advantage?

We have to do two things as a company: Keep our top line growing in the mid single digits, and grow our bottom line faster than the top.

Pepsico financials

Founded: 1965 (Pepsi-Cola and Frito-Lay merger) **Employees:** 271,000
Headquarters: Purchase, New York

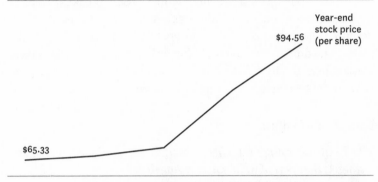

Year-end stock price (per share)

$94.56

$65.33

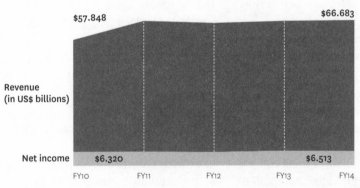

Revenue (in US$ billions)

$57.848

$66.683

Net income $6.320 $6.513

FY10   FY11   FY12   FY13   FY14

Sources: Wall Street Journal historical stock quotes and PepsiCo annual reports

Line extensions keep the base growing. And then we're always looking for hero products—the two or three big products that will drive
the top line significantly in a particular country or segment. Mountain Dew Kickstart is one of those. It's a completely different product:
higher juice content, fewer calories, new flavors. We thought about
this innovation differently. In the past we just would have created

new flavors of Mountain Dew. But Kickstart comes in a slim can and doesn't look or taste like the old Mountain Dew. It's bringing new users into the franchise: women who say, "Hey, this is an 80-calorie product with juice in a package I can walk around with." It has generated more than $200-million in two years, which in our business is hard to do.

Is this an example of design thinking, or just part of the innovation process?

There's a fine line between innovation and design. Ideally, design leads to innovation and innovation demands design. We're just getting started. Innovation accounted for 9% of our net revenue last year. I'd like to raise that to the mid teens, because I think the marketplace is getting more creative. To get there, we'll have to be willing to tolerate more failure and shorter cycles of adaptation.

Do you feel that companies have to reinvent themselves every few years, that competitive advantage is fleeting?

No question about it. It's been a long time since you could talk about sustainable competitive advantage. The cycles are shortened. The rule used to be that you'd reinvent yourself once every seven to 10 years. Now it's every two to three years. There's constant reinvention: how you do business, how you deal with the customer.

Managing Change

How do you bring everyone in the company along with what sounds like a dramatic change in approach?

The most important thing was finding the right person in Mauro. Our beverage people immediately embraced how he could help us think about product design and development. Then retailers fell in love with him and started inviting him to their shops to talk about how to reset their shelves. Mauro's team grew from about 10 people to almost 50, and we set him up in Soho in New York City. Now our products look like they're tailored to the right cohort groups, and our packaging looks pretty damn good, too.

How do you push the culture change throughout the company?

In the past, being decentralized was our strength, but also our weakness. It's a fine approach when the whole world is growing and life is peachy. But it doesn't work when things are volatile globally and you need coordination. We've given our people 24 to 36 months to adapt. I told everyone that if they don't change, I'd be happy to attend their retirement parties.

How do you measure whether or not people are making it?

We watch how they act in our global meetings and whether they include design early in the process. We see how much innovation, influenced by design, is being put into the market. We maintain an aggressive productivity program to take costs out and free up resources. You have to squeeze as much as you can out of every dollar, and we watch how many costs are coming out.

Purpose and the Portfolio

You often use the term "purpose" in talking about your business. What does that mean to you?

When I became CEO in 2006, I did a series of town hall meetings with employees. Few said they came to work for a paycheck. Most wanted to build a life, not simply gain a livelihood. And they were well aware that consumers cared about health and wellness. We realized we needed to engage our people's heads, hearts, and hands. We had to produce more products that are good for you. We had to embrace sustainability. Purpose is not about giving money away for social responsibility. It's about fundamentally changing how to make money in order to deliver performance—to help ensure that PepsiCo is a "good" company where young people want to work.

Would you be willing to accept lower profit margins to "do the right thing"? Surely, there have to be trade-offs.

Purpose doesn't hurt margins. Purpose is how you drive transformation. If you don't transform the portfolio, you're going to stop top-line growth, and margins will decline anyway. So we don't really invest in "purpose," but in a strategy to keep the company successful in the future. If we hadn't tackled certain environmental issues, especially with water, we would have lost our licenses in some countries. Now, sometimes when you're changing the culture radically, you run into problems. Transformations sometimes hit your margins or top line because things don't always go in a straight line. But if you think in terms of the life span of the company, these are just small blips.

But aren't you still selling a lot of unhealthy products?

We make a portfolio of products, some of which are "fun for you" and some of which are "good for you." We sell sugary beverages and chips, but we also have Quaker Oats, Tropicana, Naked Juice, and Izze. We're reducing the salt, sugar, and fat in the core products. And we've dialed up the good-for-you offerings because societal needs have changed.

Would you consider stopping a popular product line because it doesn't meet the good-for-you standard?

That wouldn't make sense, because none of our products is bad or unsafe. We give consumers choices that reflect their lifestyles. If you want to consume Pepsi, we'll give you Pepsi in every size possible so that on one occasion you can consume 12 ounces and on another only seven and a half. We want to make sure that both the good-for-you and the fun-for-you products are readily available, affordably priced, and great tasting. And we make sure that good-for-you tastes as good as fun-for-you. We want you to love our Quaker Oats Real Medleys as much as you love Doritos Loaded.

Do you try to push sales of the healthier products?

Yes, but we also want to preserve choice. We've taken lessons from Richard Thaler and Cass Sunstein's book *Nudge.* We try to put portion-control packages out front on the shelves. We make sure our diet products are merchandised as aspirationally as our full-sugar products are. We advertise Gatorade only with athletes in mind because it's not intended to be a recreational beverage.

PepsiCo's billion-dollar brands

Beverages	Food
Pepsi	Lay's
Mountain Dew	Doritos
Gatorade	Quaker
Tropicana	Cheetos
Diet Pepsi	Ruffles
7UP	Tostitos
Mirinda	Fritos
Lipton	Walkers Crisps
Aquafina	
Pepsi Max	
Brisk	
Sierra Mist	
Diet Mountain Dew	
Starbucks ready-to-drink beverages	

Source: PepsiCo FY14 annual report

Consumers seem very demanding these days. How do you keep up with that?

We have to make sure we're engineering our portfolio for the consumer of the future. There's nothing wrong, for example, with aspartame. But if consumers say they don't like it, we have to give them a choice. We'll offer a diet product that's aspartame-free. Similarly, there's nothing wrong with high-fructose corn syrup, but if consumers say they like real sugar, we have to offer that, too.

What's your proudest accomplishment since becoming CEO?

I took over PepsiCo just after it had a string of successful years. Then everything changed. We faced new regulatory pressures on our fun-for-you categories, and our good-for-you business wasn't fully developed. The North American market slowed down, and we weren't big enough internationally. Sales through some major U.S.

customers slowed down massively. Our key beverage competitor had done a big reset of its own, and it bounced back. We looked at ourselves and saw a decentralized, far-flung company that had to be knitted together. The culture needed to change. We had to eliminate redundancies. We had to slim down to reinvest in R&D, advertising and marketing, and new capabilities. I had a choice. I could have gone pedal to the metal, stripped out costs, delivered strong profit for a few years, and then said adios. But that wouldn't have yielded long-term success. So I articulated a strategy to the board focusing on the portfolio we needed to build, the muscles we needed to strengthen, the capabilities to develop. The board said, "We know there will be hiccups along the way, but you have our support, so go make it happen." We started to implement that strategy, and we've delivered great shareholder value while strengthening the company for the long term.

Growing up in Madras, you seem to have broken every possible stereotypical expectation of a young girl in India. Are you still that person?

To a certain extent. When you're a CEO, you can't break too many stereotypical expectations. I wish you could, but you can't. In those days, there was a well-defined conservative stereotype, so everything I did was breaking the framework. I played in a rock band. I climbed trees. I did stuff that made my parents wonder, "What the hell is she doing?" But I also was a good student and a good daughter, so I never brought shame on the family. And I was lucky that the men in my family thought the women should have an equal shot at everything. I'm still a bit of a rebel, always saying that we cannot sit still. Every morning you've got to wake up with a healthy fear that the world is changing, and a conviction that, to win, you have to change faster and be more agile than anyone else.

Originally published in September 2015. Reprint R1509F

Engineering Reverse Innovations

by Amos Winter and Vijay Govindarajan

SLOWLY BUT STEADILY, IT'S dawning on Western multinationals that it may be a good idea to design products and services in developing economies and, after adding some global tweaks, export them to developed countries.

This process, called "reverse innovation" because it's the opposite of the traditional approach of creating products for advanced economies first, allows companies to enjoy the best of both worlds. It was first described six years ago in an HBR article cowritten by one of the authors of this article, Vijay Govindarajan.

But despite the inexorable logic of reverse innovation, only a few multinationals—notably Coca-Cola, GE, Harmon, Microsoft, Nestlé, PepsiCo, Procter & Gamble, Renault, and Levi Strauss—have succeeded in crafting products in emerging markets and selling them worldwide. Even emerging giants—such as Jain Irrigation, Mahindra & Mahindra, and the Tata Group—have found it tough to create offerings that catch on in both kinds of markets.

For three years now we've been studying this challenge, analyzing more than 35 reverse innovation projects started by multinationals. Our research suggests that the problem stems from a failure to grasp the unique economic, social, and technical contexts of emerging markets. At most Western companies, product developers, who spend a lifetime creating offerings for people similar to themselves, lack a visceral understanding of emerging market consumers, whose spending habits, use of technologies, and perceptions of status are very different. Executives have trouble figuring out how to overcome the constraints of emerging markets—or take advantage of the freedoms they offer. Unable to find the way forward, they tend to fall into one or more mental traps that prevent them from successfully developing reverse innovations.

Our study also shows that executives can avoid these traps by adhering to certain design principles, which together provide a road map for reverse innovation. We distilled them partly from our work with multinationals and partly from the firsthand experiences of a team of MIT engineers led by this article's other author, Amos Winter. His team spent six years designing an off-road wheelchair for people in developing countries, which is now manufactured in India. Called the Leveraged Freedom Chair (LFC), it is 80% faster and 40% more efficient to propel than a conventional wheelchair, and it sells for approximately $250—on par with other developing world wheelchairs. The technologies that generate its high performance and low cost have been incorporated into a Western version, the GRIT Freedom Chair, which was modified with consumer feedback and sells in the United States for $3,295—less than half the price of competing products.

As we will show in the following pages, the reverse innovation process succeeds when engineering creatively intersects with strategy. Companies can capture business opportunities only when they design appropriate products or services and understand the business case for them. That's why it took two academics—one teaching mechanical engineering, and the other strategy—to come up with the principles that must guide the creation of reverse innovations.

Five Traps—and How to Avoid Them

For every product, multinational companies typically produce three variations: a top-of-the-line offering, which provides the best performance at a premium price; a "better" version, which delivers 80% of that performance at 80% of the price; and a "good" variant,

Idea in Brief

The Problem

Multinational companies are starting to realize that developing new products in and for emerging markets will allow them to outperform local rivals and undercut them on price—and even disrupt Western markets. However, most struggle to create those products and then sell them in the developed world.

The Analysis

A three-year study suggests that Western companies often fail to grasp the economic, social, and technical contexts of emerging markets. Most Western product engineers find it tough to overcome these markets' constraints and leverage their flexibility. They tend to fall into one or more traps that thwart their innovation efforts.

The Takeaways

Companies can avoid these traps if they:

1. Define the problem independent of solutions.

2. Create the optimal solution using the design flexibility available.

3. Understand the technical landscape behind the problem.

4. Test products with as many stakeholders as possible.

5. Use constraints to create global winners.

which provides 70% and costs 70% as much. To break into emerging markets, where consumers have very high expectations but much smaller pocketbooks, multinationals usually follow a design philosophy that minimizes the up-front risks: They value-engineer the "good" product, watering it down to a "fair" one that offers 50% of the performance at 50% of the price.

This rarely works. In developing countries, not only do "fair" (or "good enough") products prove too expensive for the middle class, but the upmarket consumers—who can afford them—will prefer the top-of-the-line versions. Meanwhile, because of economies of scale and the globalization of supply chains, local companies are now bringing out high-value products, at relatively cheap prices, more quickly than they used to. Consequently, most multinationals capture only small slivers of the local market.

To win over consumers in developing countries, multinationals' products and services must match or beat the performance of existing ones but at a lower cost. In other words, they must provide 100% of the performance at 10% of the price, as product developers wryly put it. Only through the creation of such disruptive products and technologies can companies both outperform local rivals and undercut them on price. But the traps we mentioned earlier prevent companies from meeting this challenge. To escape those traps, they must follow five design principles.

Trap 1: Trying to match market segments to existing products

Current offerings and processes cast a long shadow when multinationals start creating products for developing countries. At first it appears to be quicker, cheaper, and less risky to adapt an existing product than to develop one from scratch. The idea that time-tested products, with modifications, won't appeal to lower-income customers is difficult to digest. Designers struggle to get away from existing technologies.

The U.S. tractor-manufacturer John Deere, a seasoned global player, encountered this problem in India. There Deere initially sold tractors it had carefully modified for emerging markets. But its small tractors had a wide turning radius, because they had been designed for America's large farms. Indian holdings are very small and close to one another, so farmers there prefer tractors that can make narrow turns. Only after John Deere designed ab initio a tractor for the local market did it taste success in India.

Design principle 1: Define the problem independent of solutions

Casting off preconceived solutions before you set down to define problems will help your company avoid the first trap—and spot opportunities outside its existing product portfolio. Consider the problem of irrigating farms in emerging markets. Farmers will argue for the expansion of the power grid so that they can use electricity to run water pumps and irrigate fields. However, farmers need water, not electricity, and the real requirement is getting water to crops—not power to pumps. If they isolate the problem, engineers may find that creating ponds near fields or using solar-powered pumps is more cost-effective and environmentally appropriate than expanding the power grid.

When defining problems, executives must keep their eyes and ears open for behavior that may signal needs that customers haven't articulated. In 2002, Commonwealth Telecommunications Organisation researchers reported that in East Africa, people were transferring airtime to family and friends in villages, who were then using or reselling it. Doing so allowed workers in cities to get money to people back home without making long and unsafe journeys with large amounts of cash. It indicated a latent demand for money remittance services. That's how M-Pesa, the successful mobile money-transfer service, was born.

It's good to study the global market in-depth before kicking off the design process. For example, when the MIT team analyzed the wheelchair market, it learned that of the 40 million people with disabilities who didn't have wheelchairs, 70% lived in rural areas where rough roads and muddy paths were often the only links to education, employment, markets, and the community. Environmental conditions were harsh; traditional wheelchairs broke down quickly as a result and were difficult to repair. Because of their poverty, most people got wheelchairs free or at subsidized prices from NGOs, religious organizations, or government agencies. Those suppliers were willing to pay $250 to $350 for a wheelchair—an important price constraint.

No wheelchair user specified the mobility solution he or she desired; the team had to figure out the needs of the market by watching and listening. For inspiration, it drew on the numerous complaints it heard: Wheelchairs were tough to push on village roads; manually powered tricycles were too big to use indoors; imported wheelchairs couldn't be repaired in villages; the commute to an office was often more than a mile, so it was tiring. And so on.

The team's assessment of consumer needs generated four core design requirements:

1. A price of approximately $250

2. A travel range of three miles a day over varied terrain

Key advantages of the Leveraged Freedom Chair

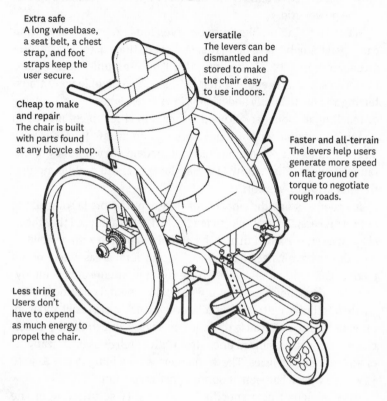

Extra safe
A long wheelbase, a seat belt, a chest strap, and foot straps keep the user secure.

Versatile
The levers can be dismantled and stored to make the chair easy to use indoors.

Cheap to make and repair
The chair is built with parts found at any bicycle shop.

Faster and all-terrain
The levers help users generate more speed on flat ground or torque to negotiate rough roads.

Less tiring
Users don't have to expend as much energy to propel the chair.

Source: GRIT/Asme Demand

3. Indoor usability and maneuverability

4. Easy, low-cost maintenance and local repair

Those criteria conveyed little about what form the wheelchair would have to take. However, had the team missed one of them, imposed an existing solution, or made its own assumptions, it probably would have failed.

Trap 2: Trying to reduce the price by eliminating features

Many multinationals think this is the way to make products afford-able for consumers in emerging markets. People in developing countries are willing to accept lower quality and products based on sunset technologies, runs the argument. This approach often leads to poor decisions and bad product designs.

For example, when one of the Big Three automobile makers decided to enter India in the mid-1990s, it charged its product devel-opers in Detroit with coming up with a suitable model. The design-ers took an existing midprice car and eliminated what they felt were unnecessary features for India, including power windows in the rear doors. The new model's price was within the reach of Indians at the top of the pyramid—who hire chauffeurs. Thus the chauffeurs got power windows up front while the owners had to hand-crank the rear windows, greatly reducing customer satisfaction.

Design principle 2: Create an optimal solution, not a watered-down one, using the design freedoms available in emerging markets

Though emerging markets have many constraints, they offer intrin-sic design freedoms as well. These freedoms take various forms: In Egypt high irradiance makes solar power attractive in areas with unreliable power; in India low labor costs and high material costs make manual fabrication cost-effective. Even behavioral differences broaden companies' options: Some African consumers prioritize the purchase of TV sets over roofs, suggesting that companies must appeal to users' wants as well as their needs.

Carefully considering design freedoms helped the MIT team achieve many objectives. For instance, wheelchairs that use a mechanical system of multiple gears, just as geared bicycles do, were available in the developing world, but they were very expen-sive, and few could afford them. Compelled to devise an alternative, the engineers homed in on people's ability to make a broad range of arm movements as something they could use in the drivetrain to make the chair go faster or slower. While that ability isn't specific to emerging markets, the engineers wouldn't have thought of using it if they weren't trying to achieve high performance at a low price—a requirement specific to emerging markets.

The MIT team designed the LFC with two long levers that are pushed to propel the chair; users change speed by shifting the position of their hands on the levers. To go up a hill, users grab high on the levers and gain more leverage; in "low gear" the levers provide 50% more torque than pushing the rims of the chair does. On a flat road, they grab low and push through a larger angle to move faster, generating speeds that are 75% faster than a standard wheelchair's. To brake, users pull back on the levers.

By making the users the machines' most complex part—they are both the power source and the gearbox—the team could fabricate the drivetrain from a simple, single-speed assembly of bicycle parts. In fact, the ability to use bicycle parts was another freedom the team could exploit. People in developing countries use bicycles extensively, and repair shops that stock spare parts are almost everywhere. Incorporating bicycle parts into the drivetrain made the LFC low cost, sustainable, and easy to repair, especially in remote villages.

Trap 3: Forgetting to think through all the technical requirements of emerging markets

When designing offerings for the developing world, engineers assume they're dealing with the same technical landscape that they are in the developed world. But while the laws of science may be the same everywhere, the technical infrastructure is very different in emerging markets. Engineers must understand the technical factors behind problems there—the physics, the chemistry, the energetics, the ecology, and so on—and conduct rigorous analyses to determine the viability of possible solutions.

Thorough calculations will allow engineers to validate or refute assumptions about the market. Consider the PlayPump, designed for Africa, which pumps water from the ground into a tower by harnessing the energy of village children pushing a merry-go-round. Having children do something useful for the community while playing is a win-win by any yardstick. Moreover, a first-order engineering analysis suggested that the technological assumptions were logical.

U.S.-focused upgrades to the GRIT Freedom Chair

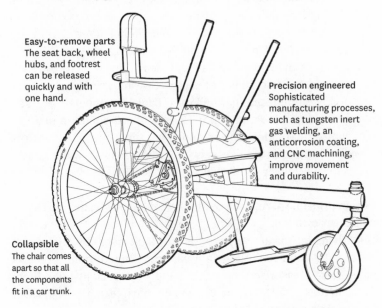

Easy-to-remove parts
The seat back, wheel hubs, and footrest can be released quickly and with one hand.

Precision engineered
Sophisticated manufacturing processes, such as tungsten inert gas welding, an anticorrosion coating, and CNC machining, improve movement and durability.

Collapsible
The chair comes apart so that all the components fit in a car trunk.

Source: GRIT/Nathan Cooke

Let's assume that in a 1,000-strong village, each person needs three liters of drinking water a day, the village has a tower that can hold 3,000 liters, and it's 10 meters high. Using high school physics, one can calculate that 25 children, playing for 10 minutes each, could theoretically fill the tower.

But further analysis alters the picture. After all, children spin merry-go-rounds so that they can ride them until they're dizzy, and if all the energy from their pushing goes to pumping water, the merry-go-round will stop as soon as they stop pushing. That's no fun! If we assume that half their energy goes into spinning and half into pumping, the energy requirement doubles; 50 children must use the PlayPump for 10 minutes each daily to keep the tower full.

If the water comes from a well 10 meters deep, double the energy will be necessary and 100 children must use the merry-go-round. Accounting for inefficiencies, the number could go to 200. What happens when it's too hot, wet, or cold, and children don't want to play on the PlayPump? How will the village get its water then? If the makers of the PlayPump had included all those factors in their calculations, they would have realized it wasn't a technically viable solution. Despite receiving the World Bank Development Marketplace award in 2000 and donor pledges of $16.4 million in 2006, PlayPumps International had stopped installing new units by 2010. The PlayPump sounded like a good idea, but a village water system needs reliable power—and ensuring that isn't child's play.

Design principle 3: Analyze the technical landscape behind the consumer problem

Underlying technical relationships may look markedly different in developing countries. For example, urban Indian homes receive water from pressurized municipal supply systems, just like those found in the United States, which ensure that if there is a leak, water goes out but contaminants can't get in. However, most Indian households use booster pumps to suck water from the municipal pipes to rooftop tanks. This suction pulls contaminants from the ground into the pipes, creating a mechanism for contamination that is not common in the United States.

Social and economic factors often drive the technical requirements for products. For instance, if a company wants to sell inexpensive tractors to low-income farmers, it must make them light; material costs determine much of a tractor's price. Engineers then must check how lowering the weight would affect the machine's performance, particularly traction and pulling force. The latter is important; in emerging markets, farmers use tractors not only to farm but for odd jobs, such as transporting people.

By studying the technical landscape, engineers can identify pain points as well as creative paths around them. Understanding the requirements for energy, force, heat transfer, and so on will illuminate novel ways of satisfying them. As noted earlier, the LFC is human powered, which eliminates the costs of a motor and an energy source. However, the design team had to figure out how users' upper body strength could provide propulsion. It did so by calculating the power and force that people could produce with their arms and the amounts needed on various kinds of terrain. Finally, the designers worked out the optimal length of the two levers so that users could travel at peak efficiency across normal terrain and have enough strength to propel their way out of trouble in harsh conditions such as mud or sand.

Trap 4: Neglecting stakeholders
Many multinationals seem to think that all they need to do to educate product designers about consumers' needs and desires is to parachute them into an emerging market for a few days; drive them around a couple of cities, villages, and slums; and allow them to observe the locals. Those perceptions will be enough to develop products that people will purchase, they assume. But nothing could be further from the truth.

Design principle 4: Test products with as many stakeholders as possible
Companies would do well to map out the entire chain of stakeholders who will determine a product's success, at the beginning of the design process. In addition to asking who the end user will be and what he or she needs, companies must consider who will make the product, distribute it, sell it, pay for it, repair it, and dispose of it. This will help in developing not just the product but also a scalable business model.

It's best to adopt the attitude that you're designing with, not for, stakeholders. If treated as equals, they're more likely to participate in the process and provide honest feedback. When you're designing a prosthetic limb, for instance, collaborate with amputees, the clinics that provide the prostheses, and the organizations that pay for them. If you're able-bodied, it doesn't matter how many doctoral degrees you've earned; you still don't know what it's like to live with a prosthetic device in a developing country.

The MIT team formed partnerships with wheelchair builders and users throughout the developing world. Those stakeholders, who provided insights on how to make the wheelchair better, easier to manufacture, more robust, and cheaper, came up with ideas for several features. The team gathered further feedback through field trials in East Africa, Guatemala, and India, conducted in conjunction with local wheelchair manufacturing and supply organizations. The tests had a huge impact, resulting in several design modifications.

Although the first prototype performed well on rough terrain in East Africa, it didn't do so well indoors. It was too wide to go through a standard doorway, which the MIT designers hadn't noticed, and it was 20 pounds heavier than rival products were. For the next iteration, tested in Guatemala, the engineers reduced the chair's width by shaping the seat closer to the user's hips, bringing the wheels closer to the frame, and using narrower tires. By conducting a structural analysis, optimizing the strength-to-weight ratio of the frame, and reducing materials wherever possible, the team also decreased the LFC's weight by 20 pounds. That version performed well indoors, but several users felt they might fall out when traversing rough terrain. So the team included foot, waist, and chest straps to secure the user to the seat in tests in India. Users rated the third version at par with conventional wheelchairs indoors and far superior outdoors.

No matter how thorough engineers are, users expose design flaws that only they can notice. For instance, of the seven major improvements users suggested, only eliminating the LFC's excess weight had been evident to the MIT team before the East African trial. It's critical to test prototypes in the field with potential users and design solutions with organizations that will disseminate the product. Remember, design is iterative; you can't get it right the first time, so be prepared to test many prototypes.

Trap 5: Refusing to believe that products designed for emerging markets could have global appeal

Western companies tend to assume that consumers in developed markets, who are brand-conscious and performance-sensitive, will never want products from emerging markets, even if their prices are lower. Executives also worry that even if those products did catch on, they could be dangerous, cannibalizing higher-priced, higher-margin offerings.

Design principle 5: Use emerging market constraints to create global winners

Before designing solutions, companies should identify the inherent constraints that will operate on the new product or service—such as low average consumer income, poor infrastructure, and limited natural resources. This list will dictate the requirements—like price, durability, and materials—that new designs must meet.

The constraints of developing countries usually force technological breakthroughs that help innovations crack global markets. The new products become platforms on which companies can add features and capabilities that will delight many tiers of consumers across the world. One example is the Logan, a car Renault designed specifically for Eastern European customers, who are price-sensitive and demand value. Launched in Romania in 2004, the Logan cost only $6,500 but offered greater size and trunk space, higher ground clearance, and more reliability than rival products. To ensure a low price, Renault used fewer parts than usual in the vehicle and manufactured it in Romania, where labor costs are relatively low.

Two years later, Renault decided to make the Logan attractive to consumers in developed markets, by adding more safety features and greater cosmetic appeal, including metallic colors. In France it sold the Logan for as much as $9,400. In Germany sales of the Logan jumped from 6,000 units to 85,000 units over a three-year period. By 2013 sales in Western Europe had reached 430,000 units—a 19% increase over 2012. Thus, while the constraints in Eastern Europe forced Renault to create a new auto design, the result was a product that delivered high value at low cost to consumers in Western Europe as well.

Something similar is happening with the LFC: Wheelchair users in the United States and Europe have noticed the media buzz about the product and want to buy it. The MIT team worked with Continuum, a Boston-based design studio, to conduct a study of what a U.S. version of the LFC could look like. The designers also tested the LFC with potential customers in the West to identify features to add. The GRIT Freedom Chair, as the developed world model is called, was designed to fit into car trunks in the United States. It also has quick-release wheels that users can remove with one hand and is made from bicycle parts available in the United States.

Although commercial production of the Freedom Chair began only in May 2015, it's on its way to success in the developed world. The venture the MIT team founded to make the chairs, Global Research Innovation and Technology, was one of four start-ups that received a diamond award at MassChallenge, the world's largest start-up competition, three years ago. In 2014, GRIT ran a Kickstarter campaign to launch the Freedom Chair, meeting its funding goal in only five days.

How the Principles Pay Off

Few companies have avoided the traps we've described as well as the global shaving products giant Gillette did when designing an offering for India. As recently as a decade ago, Gillette made most of its money in that country by catering to top-of-the-pyramid consumers with pricey products. In 2005, Procter & Gamble acquired Gillette and immediately saw an opportunity to expand market share in the country.

Prodded by its new parent, which had been in India since the early 1990s, Gillette decided to develop a product for the 400 million middle-income Indians who shave primarily with double-edge razors. It began by exploring consumer requirements. After mapping out the value chain, from steel suppliers to end users, a cross-functional team conducted ethnographic research, spending over 3,000 hours with 1,000 would-be consumers.

Gillette learned that the needs of Indian shavers differ from those of their developed world counterparts in four ways:

Affordability

The price would be a critical constraint, since Gillette's main competitor, the double-edge razor, costs just Re 1 (less than 2 cents).

Safety

Consumers in this market segment sit on the floor in the dark early-morning hours and, using a small amount of still water, wield a mirror in one hand and a razor in the other. Shaving often results in nicks and cuts, because double-edge razors don't have a protective layer between the blade and the skin.

Even so, when Gillette's product designers watched Indian men shaving, most of the men did not cut themselves. Their response was simple: "We are experts; we don't cut ourselves." However, the team concluded that shaving requires concentration; Indian shavers could not relax or talk during the process for fear of injuring themselves. Gillette had identified a latent need: Most shavers were keen to relieve the tension by using a safer razor and blade.

Ease of use

Indian men have heavier beards and thicker facial hair than most American men do, and shave less frequently, so they have to tackle longer hairs. They also like to use a lot of shaving cream. All of that leads their razors to clog up quickly. With little running water at their disposal, Indian men need razors that they can easily rinse.

Close shaves

Gillette rightly assumed that Indian men want close shaves, as men across the world do, but the difference is that they do not place a premium on time. They spend up to 30 minutes shaving, whereas U.S. men spend five to seven minutes.

To come up with a competitive product, Gillette had to relearn the science of shaving with a single blade. It found that multiple passes of a single-blade razor can achieve a close shave because of the viscoelastic nature of hair. As a blade cuts strands of hair, it also pulls them out a little from the skin. The hairs don't spring back at once; the follicles act like the mechanisms that close a screen door slowly. Because the hairs continue to protrude, the next pass of the blade can cut them a little shorter. And so on.

This process helped Gillette hit upon a valuable design freedom: It could use only a single blade in its new razor, which drastically lowered the production cost. The new razor would also need 80% fewer parts than other razors did, greatly reducing manufacturing complexity.

Gillette's engineers then had to figure out how to flatten the skin before cutting the hairs to ensure a close shave without injury. They also had to understand the mechanics of flushing out the razor by swishing it in a cup of water. Finally, they had to balance competing requirements: Small teeth at the cartridge's front were necessary to flatten the skin before it made contact with the blade, while the rear had to have an unobstructed pass-through to allow hair and shaving cream to wash out easily.

Rethinking the razor from the ground up, the Gillette team also designed a unique pivoting head. That helped the user maneuver around the curves of the face and neck, particularly under the chin—an area difficult to shave. Seeing that Indians gripped razors in numerous ways, Gillette created a bulging handle and textured it to prevent slippage.

Gillette didn't stop at designing a product specifically for India; it also built a new business model to support it. To reduce production and transportation costs, it manufactures the product at several locations. And because India's distribution infrastructure consists of millions of mom-and-pop retailers, the team designed packaging that consumers could easily spot in any store.

Over time the American company did well in this Indian segment—mainly because it didn't set out to make the cheapest razor; it strove to make a product with superior value at an ultralow cost. The Gillette Guard razor costs Rs 15 (around 25 cents)—3% as much as the company's Mach3 razor and 2% as much as its Fusion Power razor—and each refill blade costs Rs 5 (8 cents). Introduced in 2010, the innovative product has quickly gained market share: Two out of three razors sold in India today are Gillette Guards. Although

Gillette has not sold the Guard outside India yet, it embodies the promise of a successful reverse innovation.

Though most Western companies know that the business world has changed dramatically in the past 15 years, they still don't realize that its center of gravity has pretty much shifted to emerging markets. China, India, Brazil, Russia, and Mexico are all likely to be among the world's 12 largest economies by 2030, and any company that wants to remain a market leader will have to focus on consumers there. Chief executives have no choice but to start investing in the infrastructure, processes, and people needed to develop products in emerging markets. Doing so will also allow multinationals to benefit from the "frugal engineering" (as Renault's CEO Carlos Ghosn labeled it) that's possible there. Because of abundant skilled talent—especially engineers—and relatively low salaries in those countries, the costs of creating products there are often lower than in developed nations. But no amount of investment will result in portfolios of successful new products and services if companies don't follow the design principles that govern the development of reverse innovations.

Originally published in July–August 2015. Reprint R1507F

The Employer-
Led Health Care
Revolution

*by Patricia A. McDonald, Robert S. Mecklenburg, MD,
and Lindsay A. Martin*

IN THE YEARS LEADING up to 2009, Intel tried a number of popular approaches to tame its soaring health care costs. To encourage employees and their families to be more involved in the purchase of their care and aware of its actual cost, the company implemented "consumer-driven health care" offerings such as higher-deductible plans with lower premiums, tax-advantaged accounts, and tiered-provider options. To save employees time and improve access, it opened primary care clinics at Intel work sites in Oregon, New Mexico, and Arizona. It offered wellness and fitness incentives, including optional annual health checks that would reduce premiums or deductibles, health coaches, and free on-site fitness classes.

While those programs generated improvements in employee awareness, engagement, and accountability, it had become clear by 2009 that they alone would not enable Intel to solve the problem, because they didn't affect the root cause: the steadily rising cost of the care that employees and their families were receiving. Intel projected that expenditures for its 48,000 U.S. employees and their

80,000 dependents would hit $1 billion by 2012—triple the amount it spent in 2004. Intel's leaders were torn: They wanted to protect the bottom line but were reluctant to shift more of the cost to employees, concerned that it would become harder to attract and retain top talent.

One of us (Patricia McDonald) suggested another option: Intel could use its purchasing power in markets where it had operations to influence health care players—care providers, health plan administrators or insurers, and other employers—to rise above their competing self-interests and work together to redesign the local health care system. Specifically, the company would use its deep expertise in supply chain management to improve quality, remove waste, and thereby reduce costs in both the clinical and administrative sides of local health care enterprises while putting the needs of their customers—patients—at the center of everything they did.

Intel would urge the health systems to standardize work by adopting best-practice clinical processes and adapting them to their own situations. In this case, the source would be Virginia Mason Medical Center, a health system based in Seattle. It was one of several providers in the United States that employed a version of the famed Toyota Production System to make its processes "lean"—in other words, strip them of activities that did not add value and caused delays or waits in patient care. Intel would pay for the clinical processes and Virginia Mason's expertise in installing them and would train people at the local health systems to use Intel's version of TPS to adapt them. Finally, Intel would enlist its health plan administrator, Cigna, to contribute the claims data required to establish priorities and track progress.

Intel's pilot Healthcare Marketplace Collaborative (HMC) was launched in metropolitan Portland, Oregon. Over five years, it successfully implemented new clinical processes for treating six medical conditions and for screening patients for immunizations status and illnesses such as diabetes and high blood pressure. Although assessing the HMC's full impact was not easy—and in a number of cases impossible given how the experiment was designed—the results that could be measured were significant: The HMC reduced

Idea in Brief

The Problem

Like most U.S. companies in 2009, Intel faced soaring health care costs—estimated to reach $1 billion by 2012. None of the popular approaches it tried—high-deductible/low-premium plans, on-site clinics, employee wellness programs—addressed the root cause of the problem: the steadily rising cost of care.

The Solution

The company decided to tackle the problem as it would a manufacturing challenge: by using lean improvement methods to rigorously manage the quality and cost of its health care suppliers.

Intel led a health care collaborative that focused on six clinical processes for treating conditions such as diabetes and lower back pain.

The Results

The results were significant: Treatment costs of certain medical conditions fell by 24% to 49%, patients could access care and return to work faster, patient satisfaction improved, and more than 10,000 hours' worth of waste in health care suppliers' business processes was eliminated.

the direct costs of treating three of the conditions by 24% to 49%—a tremendous accomplishment in an industry where slowing the rate of cost increases is considered a major achievement.

The HMC also emphasized evidence-based care (clinical decision making backed by validated research); eliminated unnecessary care; allowed patients to access care and return to work faster; generated high levels of patient satisfaction; and cut more than 10,000 hours of waste in business processes. (See the exhibit "Measuring results.") What's more, it did all this within the confines of today's fee-for-service reimbursement system, which is widely considered a major impediment to improving the U.S. health care system.

The need to accelerate the transformation of health care in the U.S. is urgent—for both patients and employers. We have seen some hopeful signs that the tide may be turning: Thanks to the Affordable Care Act, the proportion of adult Americans without health care coverage fell to 12.9% in 2014 from 18% in 2013. And the rate of increase in U.S. health care spending has recently slowed,

Measuring results

To measure progress, the HMC chose five metrics that addressed the aim of better, faster, and more affordable care and set audacious goals: (1) 85% of patients who called for an appointment could get one within one business day; (2) 100% of patients would refer a friend to the clinic; (3) 100% of them would receive treatment in accordance with validated research; (4) 90% would meet targets for number of days to resume normal daily routines; and (5) costs of treating a condition would be lower for the new process versus the established one.

Success measures	Lower back pain	Shoulder, knee, and hip pain	Headache	Breast problems	Upper respiratory illness	Diabetes	Screening
Same-day access	93%	86%	100%	26%	100%	100%	100%
Patient satisfaction	98%	98%	92%	94%	100%	96%	96%
Evidence-based medicine	92%	81%	N/A	100%	N/A	N/A	N/A
Rapid return to function	99%	97%	N/A	42%	N/A	N/A	N/A
Savings in direct costs	23.5%	37.7%	49.1%	N/A	N/A	N/A	N/A
Initiated	2010	2010	2011	2012	2012	2013	2012
Duration	35 mos	35 mos	24 mos	38 mos	18 mos	10 mos	14 mos
No. of patients	499	343	657	86	111	47	151

Note: The six value streams were uncomplicated back pain; uncomplicated shoulder, knee, and hip pain; uncomplicated headaches (migraines); breast problems (lumps, pain, redness, discharge); uncomplicated upper respiratory illness; diabetes; screening for influenza and pneumonia immunizations and to detect illnesses such as diabetes, high blood pressure, and colon and breast cancer.

although it's hard to know whether that's simply a by-product of the Great Recession. Still, the crisis is far from over.

The Healthcare Marketplace Collaborative model has the potential to be a game changer. One of us (Lindsay Martin) led a two-year research project by the Institute for Healthcare Improvement to identify initiatives in which employers or unions, health plans, and care providers joined forces to redesign the local health care system to achieve the triple aim of improving the health of the local population, reducing the per capita cost of care, and enhancing the patient experience. Of the dozen efforts that IHI studied, the HMC model stood out in terms of its results and its potential to be replicated.

We believe that other large employers can and should follow Intel's example. As large purchasers of health services and experts in quality improvement and supplier management, corporations are uniquely positioned to drive transformation of health care in the United States.

The Birth of the Portland Collaborative

In 2007, Pat McDonald was the manager of what was then Intel's highest-performing chip factory in the world: Fab 20, in the Portland suburb of Hillsboro. While exploring how her plant might apply a lean approach to solve problems in complex engineering processes, Pat attended a conference whose speakers included another coauthor of this article, Robert Mecklenburg, of Virginia Mason.

A leader in applying lean techniques in health care, Virginia Mason had persuaded Starbucks, Aetna, and (later) other major employers to collaborate in a successful effort in Seattle to improve the processes for treating a number of conditions. The health system had done this in response to a threat by Aetna to exclude Virginia Mason from its provider network because the prices it was charging for some specialties were higher than competitors'. McDonald toured Virginia Mason's facilities and was amazed at what she saw. For instance, the flow of work in the pediatric clinic was so efficient that the waiting room was empty.

In 2009, McDonald was invited by Richard Taylor, Intel's senior vice president and director of HR, to join a committee charged with figuring out how to bring the company's health care costs under control. "Why not solve the health care problem the same way we would solve manufacturing problems?" she said. She pointed out that Intel rigorously managed its equipment suppliers, monitoring their safety, quality, and costs, but not its health care suppliers, because like most large employers outside health care, it felt it lacked the expertise.

McDonald insisted that wasn't true. She told the committee about the Seattle effort and suggested that Intel create a health care collaborative in metropolitan Portland, where its health plan covered nearly 18,000 employees and their nearly 21,000 dependents. The committee agreed, and the Healthcare Marketplace Collaborative was born. McDonald was called on to lead the initiative. She enlisted two key champions: one from HR (Taylor) and one from manufacturing (Steve Megli, a vice president of the Technology Manufacturing Group, who was interested in applying the lean approach to health care).

Mecklenburg, the leader of the Seattle initiative, was brought on as a key adviser. Previously Virginia Mason's chief of medicine, he had recently become the medical director of its new Center for Health Care Solutions, a unit formed to encourage employers to use a collaborative model with providers and health plans to drive improvements in health care.

Mecklenburg strongly believed that for the approach to spread throughout the country, employers—not health care systems or insurers—should be the driving force. He felt that on the whole, neither providers nor health plans were consistently acting in the best interests of employers or their workers. Providers' services were too costly and their quality variable. Health plans weren't reimbursing providers on the basis of quality and were willing to pay for unnecessary visits, procedures, and medicines. Without strong pressure, they would not make enough effort to provide the highest-quality, lowest-cost care possible. Although Mecklenburg was hopeful about many elements of the legislation that would become the Affordable

Care Act, he feared that it would not generate relief fast enough. He concluded that only employers, with their purchasing power, were in a position to accelerate the pace of change. McDonald's invitation to join the HMC experiment presented an opportunity to put his ideas to the test.

Let's take an in-depth look at the Healthcare Marketplace Collaborative model and the elements that were critical to its success.

1. Make Explicit What Each Player Is Bringing to the Effort

Intel initially invited Cigna; Providence Health & Services, a multistate health care system; and Tuality Healthcare, a small local system with two community hospitals, to join the collaborative. On Providence's recommendation, two state agencies, Oregon's Public Employees' Benefit Board and the Oregon Educators Benefit Board, were asked to participate in 2010. Each organization that joined the collaborative brought skills and capabilities that the others lacked and information that players in conventional health care systems rarely share for the betterment of the overall market. It was important that each group's unique value be recognized so that all team members would feel they were equals and would be motivated to fully engage. Making explicit what each player brought to the table helped forge a strong partnership, which was necessary to overcome the natural challenges and conflicts over priorities.

Employers

Intel brought a huge customer base—its employees and their families constituted a significant proportion of the health care customers in the Portland area. It also contributed its deep expertise in system engineering, improvement methodology, and supplier management. The state agencies—which together provide health care coverage and other benefits for 270,000 active and retired employees of state agencies and universities, school districts, and community colleges and their dependents—extended the endeavor's reach in the region and added another employer perspective. Perhaps more important, their involvement showed the greater community that the work was being done to benefit everyone, not just Intel employees.

Providers

Providence and Tuality each brought a unique perspective and, because of their differing sizes, were critical in demonstrating that standard, lean processes for health care could be created and applied in a range of environments. Having both providers as part of the initiative also broadened access for employees and accommodated their preferences for big or small institutions.

Insurers or administrators

Cigna played a limited but crucial role: It provided the claims data essential for identifying which conditions should be priorities, establishing baselines for improvement efforts, and tracking progress—something that insurers and administrators generally don't do. Cigna's involvement ensured that patients' privacy rights would not be violated. It should be noted that while the information shed light on the costs and utilization of health care in the region, it was raw data. Intel had to hire a third-party vendor to analyze the data and turn it into actionable information.

Physician leader

Keenly aware that it had limited knowledge of health care, Intel felt it needed a hands-on adviser to help guide the initiative, so it asked Mecklenburg to serve as physician leader. He was an expert in applying lean techniques to health care, and as a clinician, he would be effective in explaining the approach to the care providers and getting them to engage.

The role of physician leader is critical in an employer-led collaborative. Candidates may come from inside or outside a participating health system. They must have a track record in leading change and be advocates of collaborative decision making. And they must be driven by dissatisfaction with the current state of medicine and the belief that care provider organizations today are wasting employers' and taxpayers' money and are not doing their level best for patients.

Among all the players in a collaborative, the anchor should be the employer. In many cases it will be a large corporation, but state governments, pressured by their tight budgets, are also ideal. (The ongoing Bree Collaborative in Washington State is a good example.) The founding employer can invite other like-minded employers, providers, and health plans to come to the table. Upon seeing the results, additional employers may seek to join the effort—or begin to purchase health care differently.

Such an endeavor must be organized as a serious enterprise, not treated as an "extracurricular activity" that employees have to squeeze into their already-full workloads. It requires significant personnel resources. Management and operating teams are needed to bring the stakeholders together and establish a healthy operating rhythm. (For a look at how the HMC was staffed and organized, see the exhibit "Building a collaborative.")

2. Establish a Shared Aim

The purchase of health care services for employees is often a game in which each player—employer, payer, or health care provider—tries to use its market power to secure the best deal for itself in annual negotiations. Payers (insurers or third-party administrators) attempt to wrangle discounts from providers. Providers strive to raise prices independent of cost or quality. Payers and employers try to shift actuarial risk—the risk that the assumptions built into models for pricing insurance policies may turn out to be wrong—to providers. And to offset rising costs, employers force workers to pay more for premiums and shoulder higher deductibles and copays.

Making matters worse, little information is shared among key local players. Health plans and providers often shut employers out of the discussion of costs. Health plans may be contractually prohibited from disclosing negotiated rates with providers. And although progress in getting health systems to share learning has been made via government and nonprofit initiatives, providers within a given market rarely share data on outcomes. The grand result is a system in which it is rare for all the local players to work together in a

Building a collaborative

The Healthcare Marketplace Collaborative was organized and staffed as an important business enterprise with a regular operating rhythm, not as an "extracurricular" activity.

Team	Members	Frequency	Responsibility
Core operating team	Program managers, lean experts, clinicians, and the physician leader	Weekly	Oversee the design and implementation of value streams, manage integration among the teams, identify issues such as variations in practices and data collection problems, and determine possible solutions.
Medical team	Medical directors from Intel and the two health systems, the physician leader, and program managers	Monthly	Review and modify the clinical value streams to accommodate local needs, evaluate results of various approaches, and approve the final value streams. Cultivate buy-in from skeptical clinicians and foster a patient-centric, data-driven culture.
Steering committee	Executive sponsors, medical directors, and the physician leader	Quarterly	Set the initiative's strategic direction, determine how many and what type of conditions should be tackled, and monitor progress.
All-hands team	All key players; other stakeholders such as clinicians and IT staff from the health systems	Annually	Conduct annual planning and align strategic direction.

What did it take to staff the HMC initiative? Here's how the resource allocation broke down.

Company	Members of the HMC	Commitment (% of time per person)
Intel	Executive sponsors: VP of human resources, VP of manufacturing	10%
	Medical director	20%
	Program manager: midlevel manager with experience in leading lean projects and managing initiatives across organizations	50%
	Operations facilitators: 2 to 3 senior individual contributors skilled in group facilitation and long-range planning	30%
	Lean experts: 2 to 4 people certified in lean methodologies	50% to 75%
	Administrative assistant	15%
	HMC champions: 2 senior VPs	1%
	Data specialist	20%
Providence and Tuality	Executive sponsors: Providence's chief strategy officer and Tuality's CEO	10% to 15%
	Medical directors	20%
	Program/operations managers	40%
	Clinicians: data collection, training, and process development, as well as clinical care	50%
Public employers	Executive sponsor: administrator of the boards	3% to 5%
Virginia Mason	Physician leader	5%
Cigna	Executive sponsor: regional medical executive	5%
	Data analyst	5%

transparent way to improve the quality and cost of health care and enhance the patient experience.

To break this dynamic, the HMC's members agreed to focus on an aim that would be in the interests of all the stakeholders, including patients: providing the right care in the right place at the right time and the right cost for Intel employees and families and all other Portland-area health care users. They would strive to eliminate waste, achieve zero defects, and, where possible, focus on keeping people well, reducing the need for reactive care.

When Intel approached Tuality and Providence about joining the collaborative, each asked—reacting to past experiences with employers—"Does Intel want a separate system for its employees alone?" Intel realized that would undercut the goal of establishing a shared aim and responded with a resounding no. Creating special care for Intel employees would not be beneficial for the health care providers: It could result in parallel clinical and business work processes, which would be inefficient and, in health care, could lead to an increase in "adverse events or errors"—patient injuries due to medical interventions rather than to underlying medical conditions. Moreover, a separate system might limit employees' choices and would not be in the best interests of the greater community.

3. Don't Reinvent the Wheel

Rather than develop new protocols from scratch, the HMC's two health systems accepted Intel's proposal to start out by acquiring proven clinical content and work processes—or, to use lean lingo, "value streams"—and quality metrics from Virginia Mason, whose lean clinical processes were evidence based and focused on the patient, addressing convenience, rapid access, cost, patients' lifestyles, and family considerations as well as quality of care. All this appealed to Intel, which was accustomed to finding the best in the industry and buying it. Intel opted to cover the full price of the value streams, because it believed they would benefit its employees and accelerate the standardization of care in the health systems. Intel also provided training for employees at the health systems in using its proprietary Rapid Integrated Lean version of the Toyota Production System to adapt the Virginia Mason processes to fit their own contexts.

Employer-led collaboratives can draw on a number of sources of processes and expertise. For example, Bellin Health Care Systems, in Wisconsin works directly with employers to drive down costs; ThedaCare, which is also in Wisconsin, offers courses and direct coaching on lean health systems and improvement methodologies; and Salt Lake City–based Intermountain Healthcare, well known for standardizing care, teaches courses in health care quality improvement.

4. Make It Flexible

No two health care providers are exactly the same in terms of size, structure, and operations. In some instances, a provider may already have an effective method of treating a targeted condition. In others, internal or structural issues (physical space, available resources, state regulations) may make it difficult, if not impossible, to simply install a clinical process without changes.

Recognizing this, the collaborative agreed at the outset that Providence and Tuality would each decide whether or how to adopt each of the new clinical processes. For example, some of them called for tasks to be performed by an advanced registered nurse practitioner who had earned at least a master's degree. Because that role did not exist in either organization at the time, Tuality and Providence had to adjust the value streams to have other personnel perform those tasks. In the end, Tuality chose to adopt some form of all the value streams. Providence adopted four but decided that its programs for upper respiratory illness, diabetes, and screening were robust and would be kept; it was still committed, however, to achieving HMC goals for all three.

Proposed changes to any of the Virginia Mason value streams were vetted at meetings of Intel's global medical director, Donald C. Fisher, MD; Providence's and Tuality's medical directors; and the physician leader. The directors evaluated all the changes by testing and monitoring the results and then reconvened to reflect on how each health system could improve.

5. Prioritize on the Basis of Impact and Difficulty

Intel combed through Cigna's claims data and chose which medical conditions to focus on initially—those whose improvement would most benefit its employees, their dependents, and the company. About two years into the effort, the medical directors at Providence and Tuality selected additional conditions. The group used four criteria to establish priorities:

Expenditures and impact on patients

Intel focused on types of care on which it spent a lot of money and treated the most patients—both Intel's employees and the community at large. Although the treatment costs for certain conditions are relatively low, they typically result in greater total expenditures because they occur so frequently. Therefore, team members considered frequency as well as cost in setting priorities.

Level of complication and risk

Intel chose to start with less complicated and less risky conditions to make it easier for Providence and Tuality to put the new clinical processes in place. For example, because of their complexity and the intense emotions that patients and their families typically experience, the collaborative's steering committee opted not to tackle pregnancy or cancer while in learning mode. In addition, Intel knew from experience that tackling the most complicated challenges first—something teams are often tempted to do because the potential payoff is the highest—increases the likelihood that a program will bog down or fail.

Ease of standardization

Intel wanted processes that could be standardized easily across multiple care-delivery systems. So it initially chose value streams that Virginia Mason had already developed and successfully implemented in several health care sites.

Benefit to the health systems

Although Intel set the initial priorities, it recognized that all the stakeholders needed to benefit from implementation of the value stream. Certain "production" costs for the two health systems would be reduced by eliminating unnecessary procedures (such as MRI scans), optimizing staff (for example, using clinical professionals other than physicians to diagnose and treat uncomplicated conditions), and reengineering administrative processes. Revenue would grow as a result of increasing patient throughput—for example, by offering patients with uncomplicated conditions rapid access to treatment and by providing patients with complicated conditions rapid access to specialists (whose schedules were no longer filled by patients with uncomplicated conditions). The benefits of increased volume and reduced costs would more than offset any reduction in revenue associated with eliminating unnecessary care. Indeed, the health care providers would most likely increase their market share as better outcomes and lower costs translated into a stronger financial position.

Uncomplicated back pain was selected as the first value stream to improve because it was high on Intel's list in terms of frequency and total cost; Virginia Mason had used this lean process to treat thousands of back patients since 2005 and had solid experience standardizing the clinical process at multiple sites; and Providence and Tuality treated a high number of patients with the condition. (See the exhibit "Two approaches to treating back pain" for more on the redesigned value stream.)

6. Choose Simple Metrics and Goals

U.S. health care providers measure more than 100 indicators of the quality of their clinical processes—such as the rate of ventilator-associated pneumonia, the percentage of patients whose

Two approaches to treating back pain

Evidence shows that most patients with uncomplicated lower back pain can be treated effectively with physical therapy. Yet most health care providers routinely require more-elaborate processes that waste time and money.

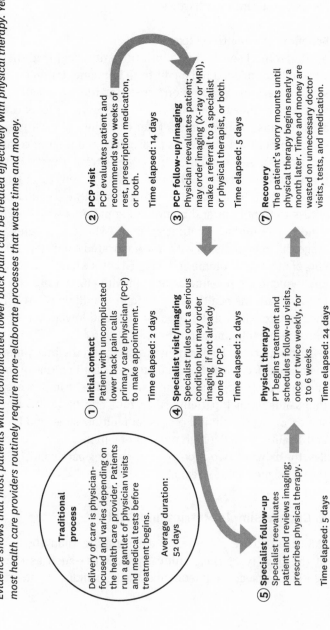

Traditional process

Delivery of care is physician-focused and varies depending on the health care provider. Patients run a gantlet of physician visits and medical tests before treatment begins.

Average duration: 52 days

① Initial contact
Patient with uncomplicated lower back pain calls primary care physician (PCP) to make appointment.

Time elapsed: 2 days

② PCP visit
PCP evaluates patient and recommends two weeks of rest, prescription medication, or both.

Time elapsed: 14 days

③ PCP follow-up/imaging
Physician reevaluates patient; may order imaging (X-ray or MRI), make a referral to a specialist or physical therapist, or both.

Time elapsed: 5 days

④ Specialist visit/imaging
Specialist rules out a serious condition but may order imaging if not already done by PCP.

Time elapsed: 2 days

⑤ Specialist follow-up
Specialist reevaluates patient and reviews imaging; prescribes physical therapy.

Time elapsed: 5 days

Physical therapy
PT begins treatment and schedules follow-up visits, once or twice weekly, for 3 to 6 weeks.

Time elapsed: 24 days

⑦ Recovery
The patient's worry mounts until physical therapy begins nearly a month later. Time and money are wasted on unnecessary doctor visits, tests, and medication.

The HMC's process

In this evidence-based process, patients feel better sooner, the cost of care is reduced, and a greater volume of people can be treated. Physicians and specialists are freed up to treat patients with more serious conditions.

Average duration: 22 days

① **Initial contact**
Patient with uncomplicated lower back pain calls DirectLine to Health Care.

Time elapsed: 0 days

② **Screening**
Rehab office assistant uses a screening tool to determine whether patient can go straight to physical therapy. If so, patient is scheduled for an evaluation within 24 hours.

Time elapsed: 1 day

③ **Physical therapy**
Physical therapist screens patient a second time for serious conditions, addresses fears (of cancer, permanent disability, the need for surgery, and so on), and begins treatment: PT visits, once a week (supplemented by home exercises), for 3 weeks.

Time elapsed: 21 days

④ **Recovery**
Patient receives reassurance immediately and starts feeling better physically within a week. If patient does not improve as expected, an appointment with a specialist is arranged.

prophylactic antibiotics are discontinued within 24 hours of surgery, and so on—which they report to public- and private-sector bodies. Although they are all valid quality indicators, few are useful in an employer-driven initiative like the HMC. The collaborative needed a set of simple, standard metrics to measure progress; it chose five that had been adopted by the Seattle collaborative and addressed the aim of better, faster, and more-affordable care. And it set audacious goals for each.

Better care
The HMC used two metrics for this goal. One gauged medical quality: whether or not patients received evidence-based care. The other tracked patient satisfaction: the proportion of patients who responded "probably" or "definitely" to the survey question "Based on today's visit, would you refer a friend to our medical clinic?" The goal for both measures was 100%.

Faster care
The HMC choose two metrics here: same-day access to care and return to function (how many days before patients could resume their normal daily routines). The goal was that 85% of patients who called Monday through Friday could get an appointment with an appropriate provider within one business day of their call. For the return-to-function metric, the team members from Intel, the medical directors from the two health systems, and the physician leader determined the targets for each value stream. The goal was for 90% of patients to meet or beat the target.

More-affordable care
The first metric for affordable care was the total cost to employer and patient of treating a condition—in other words, the fees paid to providers. (Historically, this has been hard to calculate in the United States because most providers charge for each item or service, not for the full treatment of the condition.) The collaborative compared costs from when the need for care arose and when the problem was resolved using both the new approach and the one typically used in

the health system. The goal was to actually *reduce* costs (no numerical target was set), not just slow the rate of increase.

Although not calculated in dollar figures, the return-to-function metric also was considered in gauging progress on more-affordable care. The cost of lost productivity often is much greater than the cost of care—and is something that health systems in the United States typically don't consider.

There were inevitably differences of opinion about how to implement value streams, and using common measures allowed the health systems to test approaches in parallel and easily compare the results, accelerating decisions. For example, Virginia Mason's process called for a physician and a physical therapist to jointly evaluate whether a patient whose lower back pain seems to be uncomplicated might have something more serious. Specialist physicians at both Providence and Tuality believed that the therapist alone would suffice. So the two systems tested the approach for three months—Tuality with a physician and Providence without. Recovery rates and satisfaction levels were essentially the same, so both health systems decided that physician involvement was unnecessary.

7. Use One Improvement Methodology

Getting all the members of a collaborative to agree to use the same improvement methodology is essential. The good news is that virtually any quality improvement approach can be applied, including varieties of the Toyota Production System, Six Sigma, and the Model for Improvement (created by Associates in Process Improvement and used by the Institute for Healthcare Improvement). Intel's Rapid Integrated Lean, or RIL, approach had many benefits, especially its pace: It was designed to deliver exceptional results in three weeks. It does this by focusing individuals, teams, or managers on standardizing work that is under their control and by concentrating them on problems where they can make the most impact. Intel loaned the HMC several of its lean experts and trained 48 people at Providence and Tuality in the technique. In exchange, Intel required that both providers share results with everyone in the collaborative.

In using RIL to tailor and implement the Virginia Mason processes, a core HMC operating team and specialist clinicians from the two health systems mapped out each value stream on a wall for everyone to see. People from Providence and Tuality provided input on how the workflow would fit into each of the organizations. They highlighted differences in practice and explained why each was needed. The medical directors then agreed on which changes to test.

As the work progressed, the core operating team tested pieces of the value stream (including proposed variations), observed them in action, gleaned insights, and tried again—continually learning and sharing best practices. All changes to the existing workflow were tested in small experiments and then gradually scaled up—an approach that helped get buy-in from people in the health systems. Every week the core operating team met and used Post-it notes to document what had been accomplished and what hadn't, what could be done differently, and what barriers had been encountered. It typically took 10 to 14 weeks to design and test a clinical value stream and get it ready to be implemented more broadly. Value streams for administrative processes took three to five weeks.

In addition to serving as a tracking mechanism, the visual representation of the work was a team-building exercise. Everyone learned how to work together and how efforts were progressing across all players in the system.

8. Fix the Business Side

Administrative costs consume an enormous chunk of the money that goes to health care—more than 25% of U.S. hospitals' expenditures, according to a 2014 analysis by David Himmelstein and colleagues published in *Health Affairs.* So any serious effort to make health care more affordable has to tackle not only the clinical side but also the business side. In addition, administrative processes such as booking appointments and billing have a significant impact on the patient experience.

The HMC used RIL to remove waste and non-value-adding activities from Providence's and Tuality's business operations, including billing, inventory management, checking in patients, processes for getting patients into rooms to be treated, and cleaning. As of March 2014, a total of 48 business processes had been improved at the two systems, generating an estimated $2.6 million in annual savings. Since then, both have continued their improvement efforts.

Understanding the Challenges

Naturally, the Healthcare Marketplace Collaborative encountered challenges. As the anchor of the initiative, Intel brought the group together, implemented RIL, and drove players to abide by the process. Sometimes people at the other member organizations resented being told what to do, so Intel had to be careful not to push too hard.

Persuading clinicians in the health care systems to accept standard clinical processes wasn't always easy. At Intel, if a manufacturing process was deemed an improvement or a best practice, it was documented and then implemented at all the company's factories. There were specific methods and procedures for putting new process steps in place. This was not the case at the health systems. Not all clinicians, even within a specialty, practiced the same way; standard protocols often hadn't been instituted. Some medical leaders of clinics and individual care providers didn't like being told what was best for their patients. The collaborative had to find a balance between allowing highly trained clinicians to use their judgment in unique cases and creating standard approaches for treating the vast majority of patients. In addition, the health systems differed in their willingness to make changes that would reduce office visits with a physician and, as a result, their reimbursements.

The medical directors on the HMC team played an instrumental role in overcoming such resistance. Launching value-stream efforts at Providence and Tuality clinics and then demonstrating the results also proved effective in getting people at other sites on board. Ultimately, embedding protocols proven to provide the best care in an electronic-medical-record system will help clinicians stick with them. Virginia Mason already does this. For example, its clinicians cannot order an MRI for lower back pain unless they identify a medical indication for it in the EMR system or phone a designated expert.

Persuading patients to abide by the new process also requires a concerted effort. For instance, the health systems couldn't force patients with uncomplicated back pain to go directly to a clinic and not see their primary care physicians first. Intel and the two state agencies understood this and used a number of means to publicize the streamlined services and encourage people to use them. Still, it takes time to change mindsets.

Sometimes the health systems lacked sufficient staff to implement a new value stream smoothly. For instance, staff turnover and difficulty lining up surgeons and radiologists explain why same-day access for the breast problems value stream was so low. Viewing those poor results as an improvement opportunity, Tuality decided to dedicate another surgeon to the breast problems value stream.

Another big challenge was getting data. In a number of cases, the health systems lacked the resources to track metrics; in others, it was difficult to track particular kinds of patients, such as unemployed Medicare patients. Cigna provided the cost data, but there was a frustrating lag of several months because the insurer had to wait for claims to be submitted, approved, and paid. In other industries, gathering cost data takes minutes or even seconds. (These slow data turns—the norm in the health care industry—are a major barrier to rapid improvements in clinical processes.) For some value streams, the HMC couldn't get meaningful cost data because it had such information only for Intel employees and the number treated by the new value stream was too small to draw statistically valid conclusions. Because of the challenges in getting useful data, it's wise to bring a data analysis engineer on board early in the development stage of a value stream.

Finally, agreeing on a uniform set of medical classification codes was difficult. More than 16,000 codes for diagnoses and procedures are used for billing and reimbursement in the United States. Back pain, for example, has many possible codes, and preferences may differ by provider. The medical directors ultimately decided to use the codes in Virginia Mason's handbooks to conduct cost analyses. But differences between the codes used for existing clinical processes and those used for the new ones made it difficult, if not impossible, to compare results. For the other metrics, the HMC did not use control groups to measure the degree of improvement. Instead, it created extremely ambitious goals and tried, where it could, to use them to gauge progress.

———————

The Healthcare Marketplace Collaborative ended in June 2014, after the improvement process had been established at both health systems and Intel was no longer needed to drive the effort. While results of the HMC experiment were hardly perfect, and should be viewed as coming from a challenging work in progress rather than from an ideal end state, they proved that an employer can engage all the players in a market to accelerate health care reform. HMC's focus on patient-centered care produced solid cost savings and, more important, behavioral changes grounded in evidence-based medicine, measures, results, and patient satisfaction.

Intel is now applying elements of the HMC approach to purchasing health care services in Oregon and New Mexico and plans to do so elsewhere as well.

The Bree Collaborative, in Washington State, in which Bob Mecklenburg is involved, is taking the Portland approach to the next level. It incorporates goals and metrics like those used in Portland in employers' contracts with participating health systems, but it involves more employers and health systems, is tackling more-complicated conditions, and has created or is creating a standard bundle of all the services that patients with a given condition require through recovery. Each employer negotiates a fixed price for each bundle, which also includes a warranty against hospital readmissions for avoidable complications. The initiative has already created bundles for joint replacements and lumbar fusion and expects to complete one for coronary artery bypass grafting in the summer of 2015.

We encourage employers to use their purchasing power to drive the transformation of health care in their regions. That means taking the lead in securing better health for local populations, improving their experiences of care, and lowering costs for employees and companies. Employers should choose plans and providers on the basis of their willingness to join them in the effort. Ultimately, companies in such initiatives should report the results of health systems' efforts to make care better, faster, and more affordable and encourage employees to use the information to select providers.

We urge care providers to join collaboratives in their regions and develop business models in which better outcomes and lower costs translate into improved financial performance. Providers should build new skills to standardize clinical and business processes and strive to integrate all aspects of care, including behavioral or mental health and social services. They should learn to be transparent about prices and outcomes to help employees choose the best providers and to help employers teach their employees that more care is not necessarily better care.

Health plans should develop business models that allow them to succeed in an environment in which health care costs and premiums are decreasing. They should identify high-performing providers of care or those on a positive trajectory. They should make information on providers' prices and outcomes rapidly available to employers, employees, and their families in a useful form. They should lend their power and insight to efforts to change the payment system so that it is no longer an obstacle to improving outcomes and lowering costs.

In virtually all regions, at least some employers, providers, and health plans will be able to transcend narrow self-interest and cooperate to develop new business models that result in the best health outcomes for individuals at lowest cost. We enthusiastically invite them to join us on the journey.

Originally published in July–August 2015. Reprint R1507B

Getting to *Sí, Ja, Oui, Hai,* and *Da*

by Erin Meyer

TIM CARR, AN AMERICAN working for a defense company based in the midwestern United States, was about to enter a sensitive bargaining session with a high-level Saudi Arabian customer, but he wasn't particularly concerned. Carr was an experienced negotiator and was well-trained in basic principles: Separate the people from the problem. Define your BATNA (best alternative to a negotiated agreement) up front. Focus on interests, not positions. He'd been there, read that, and done the training.

The lengthy phone call to Saudi Arabia proceeded according to plan. Carr carefully steered the would-be customer to accept the deal, and it seemed he had reached his goal. "So let me just review," he said. "You've agreed that you will provide the supplies for next year's project and contact your counterpart at the energy office to get his approval. I will then send a letter. . . . Next you've said that you will. . . ." But when Carr finished his detailed description of who had agreed to what, he was greeted with silence. Finally a soft but firm voice said, "I told you I would do it. You think I don't keep my promises? That I'm not good on my word?"

That was the end of the discussion—and of the deal.

The many theories about negotiation may work perfectly when you're doing a deal with a company in your own country. But in today's globalized economy you could be negotiating a joint venture in China, an outsourcing agreement in India, or a supplier contract in Sweden. If so, you might find yourself working with very different norms of communication. What gets you to "yes" in one culture gets you to "no" in another. To be effective, a negotiator must have a sense of how his counterpart is reacting. Does she want to cooperate? Is she eager, frustrated, doubtful? If you take stock of subtle messages, you can adjust your own behavior accordingly. In an international negotiation, however, you may not have the contextual understanding to interpret your counterpart's communication—especially unspoken signals—accurately. In my work and research, I find that when managers from different parts of the world negotiate, they frequently misread such signals, reach erroneous conclusions, and act, as Tim Carr did, in ways that thwart their ultimate goals.

In the following pages, I draw on my work on cross-cultural management to identify five rules of thumb for negotiating with someone whose cultural style of communication differs from yours. The trick, as we will see, is to be aware of key negotiation signals and to adjust both your perceptions and your actions in order to get the best results.

1. Adapt the Way You Express Disagreement

In some cultures it's appropriate to say "I totally disagree" or to tell the other party he's wrong. This is seen as part of a normal, healthy discussion. A Russian student of mine told me, "In Russia we enter the negotiation ready for a great big debate. If your Russian counterpart tells you passionately that he completely disagrees with every point you have made, it's not a sign that things are starting poorly. On the contrary, it's an invitation to a lively discussion."

In other cultures the same behavior would provoke anger and possibly an irreconcilable breakdown of the relationship. An American manager named Sean Green, who had spent years negotiating partnerships in Mexico, told me that he quickly learned that if he wanted to make progress toward a deal, he needed to say things like "I do not quite understand your point" and "Please explain more why you think that." If he said, "I disagree with that," the discussions might shut down completely.

Idea in Brief

The Problem

In cross-border negotiations, managers often discover that perfectly rational deals fall apart when their counterparts make what seem to be unreasonable demands or don't respect their commitments.

Why It Happens

Each culture has its own communication norms, and over time you'll find that what gets you to "yes" in one culture may get you to "no" in another.

The Solution

You can reduce miscommunication by respecting these five rules of thumb:

1. Figure out how to express disagreement.
2. Recognize what emotional expressiveness signifies.
3. Learn how the other culture builds trust.
4. Avoid yes-or-no questions.
5. Beware of putting it in writing.

The key is to listen for verbal cues—specifically, what linguistics experts call "upgraders" and "downgraders." Upgraders are words you might use to strengthen your disagreement, such as "totally," "completely," "absolutely." Downgraders—such as "partially," "a little bit," "maybe"—soften the disagreement. Russians, the French, Germans, Israelis, and the Dutch use a lot of upgraders with disagreement. Mexicans, Thai, the Japanese, Peruvians, and Ghanaians use a lot of downgraders.

Try to understand upgraders and downgraders within their own cultural context. If a Peruvian you're negotiating with says he "disagrees a little," a serious problem may well be brewing. But if your German counterpart says he "completely disagrees," you may be on the verge of a highly enjoyable debate.

2. Know When to Bottle It Up or Let It All Pour Out

In some cultures it's common—and entirely appropriate—during negotiations to raise your voice when excited, laugh passionately, touch your counterpart on the arm, or even put a friendly arm around him. In other cultures such self-expression not only feels intrusive or surprising but may even demonstrate a lack of professionalism.

What makes international negotiations interesting (and complicated) is that people from some very emotionally expressive cultures—such as Brazil, Mexico, and Saudi Arabia—may also avoid open disagreement. (See the exhibit "Preparing to face your counterpart.") Mexicans tend to disagree softly yet express emotions openly. As a Mexican manager, Pedro Alvarez, says, "In Mexico we perceive emotional expressiveness as a sign of honesty. Yet we are highly sensitive to negative comments and offended easily. If you disagree with me too strongly, I would read that as a signal that you don't like me."

In other cultures—such as Denmark, Germany, and the Netherlands—open disagreement is seen as positive as long as

Preparing to face your counterpart

The map below sorts nationalities according to how confrontational and emotionally expressive they are. Although negotiators often believe that the two characteristics go hand in hand, that's not always the case.

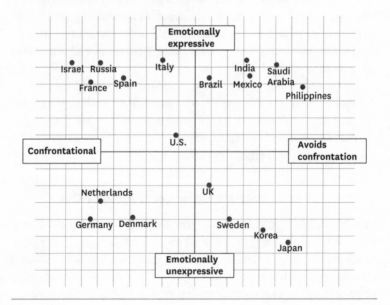

it is expressed calmly and factually. A German negotiator, Dirk Firnhaber, explains that the German word *Sachlichkeit,* most closely translated in English as "objectivity," refers to separating opinions from the person expressing them. If he says, "I totally disagree," he means to debate the opinions, not disapprove of the individual.

People from cultures like these may view emotional expressiveness as a lack of maturity or professionalism in a business context. Firnhaber tells a story about one deal he negotiated with a French company. It began calmly enough, but as the discussion continued, the French managers grew animated: "The more we discussed, the more our French colleagues became emotional—with voices raised, arms waving, ears turning red . . . the whole thing." Firnhaber was increasingly uncomfortable with the conversation and at times thought the deal would fall apart. To his surprise, the French took a very different view: "When the discussion was over, they seemed delighted with the meeting, and we all went out for a great dinner."

So the second rule of international negotiations is to recognize what an emotional outpouring (whether yours or theirs) signifies in the culture you are negotiating with, and to adapt your reaction accordingly. Was it a bad sign that the Swedish negotiators sat calmly across the table from you, never entered into open debate, and showed little passion during the discussion? Not at all. But if you encountered the same behavior while negotiating in Israel, it might be a sign that the deal was about to die an early death.

3. Learn How the Other Culture Builds Trust

During a negotiation, both parties are explicitly considering whether the deal will benefit their own business and implicitly trying to assess whether they can trust each other. Here cultural differences hit us hard. How we come to trust someone varies dramatically from one part of the world to another.

Consider this story from John Katz, an Australian negotiating a joint venture in China. Initially, he felt he was struggling to get the information his side needed, so he asked his company's China consultant for advice. The consultant suggested that Katz was going at the deal too quickly and should spend more time building trust. When Katz said he'd been working hard to do just that by supplying a lot of information from his side and answering all questions transparently, the consultant replied, "The problem is that you need to approach them from a relationship perspective, not a business perspective. You won't get what you want unless you develop trust differently."

Research in this area divides trust into two categories: *cognitive* and *affective*. Cognitive trust is based on the confidence you feel in someone's accomplishments, skills, and reliability. This trust comes from the head. In a negotiation it builds through the business interaction: You know your stuff. You are reliable, pleasant, and consistent. You demonstrate that your product or service is of high quality. I trust you. Affective trust arises from feelings of emotional closeness, empathy, or friendship. It comes from the heart. We laugh together, relax together, and see each other on a personal level, so I feel affection or empathy for you. I trust you.

In a business setting, the dominant type of trust varies dramatically from one part of the world to another. In one research project, Professor Roy Chua, of Singapore Management University, surveyed Chinese and American executives from a wide range of industries, asking them to list up to 24 important members of their professional networks. He then asked them to indicate the extent to which they felt comfortable sharing their personal problems and dreams with each of those contacts. "These items showed an affective-based willingness to depend on and be vulnerable to the other person," Chua explains. Finally, participants were asked to indicate how reliable, competent, and knowledgeable each contact was. These assessments showed a more cognitive-based willingness to depend on the other person.

The survey revealed that in negotiations (and business in general) Americans draw a sharp line between cognitive and affective trust. American culture has a long tradition of separating the emotional from the practical. Mixing the two risks conflict of interest and is viewed as unprofessional. Chinese managers, however, connect the two, and the interplay between cognitive and affective trust is much stronger. They are quite likely to develop personal bonds where they have financial or business ties.

In most emerging or newly emerged markets, from BRIC to Southeast Asia and Africa, negotiators are unlikely to trust their counterparts until an affective connection has been made. The same is true for most Middle Eastern and Mediterranean cultures. That may make negotiations challenging for task-oriented Americans, Australians, Brits, or Germans. Ricardo Bartolome, a Spanish manager, told me that he finds Americans to be very friendly on the surface, sometimes surprisingly so, but difficult to get to know at a deeper level. "During a negotiation they are so politically correct and careful not to show negative emotion," he said. "It makes it hard for us to trust them."

So in certain cultures you need to build an affective bond or emotional connection as early as possible. Invest time in meals and drinks (or tea, karaoke, golf, whatever it may be), and don't talk about the deal during these activities. Let your guard down and show your human side, including your weaknesses. Demonstrate genuine interest in the other party and make a friend. Be patient: In China, for example, this type of bond may take a long time to build. Eventually, you won't have just a friend; you'll have a deal.

4. Avoid Yes-or-No Questions

At some point during your negotiation you'll need to put a proposal on the table—and at that moment you will expect to hear whether or not the other side accepts. One of the most confounding aspects of international negotiations is that in some cultures the word "yes" may be used when the real meaning is no. In other cultures "no" is the most frequent knee-jerk response, but it often means "Let's discuss further." In either case, misunderstanding the message can lead to a waste of time or a muddled setback.

A recent negotiation between a Danish company and its Indonesian supplier provides a case in point. One of the Danish executives wanted reassurance that the Indonesians could meet the desired deadline, so he asked them directly if the date was feasible.

Look for Cultural Bridges

THERE'S NO SUBSTITUTE for learning all you can about the culture you will be negotiating with. But taking a cultural bridge—someone who is from the other culture, has a foot in both cultures, or, at the very least, knows the other culture intimately—to the negotiating table will give you a head start.

Of course, if one party doesn't speak English well, it's common to have the help of a translator; but a cultural bridge can make a huge impact even if no linguistic divide exists. During breaks in the negotiation, for example, you can ask this person to interpret what's going on between the lines.

The British executive Sarah Stevens was leading a U.S. team negotiating a deal in Japan. The Japanese parties all spoke English well, but three hours into the negotiation Stevens realized that her team was doing 90% of the talking, which worried her. She asked a colleague from her company's Japan office for advice. He explained that the Japanese often pause to think before speaking—and that they don't find silence uncomfortable the way Americans or the British do. He advised Stevens to adopt the Japanese approach: After asking a question, wait patiently and quietly for an answer. He also told her that the Japanese often make decisions in groups, so they might need to confer before giving an answer. If after a period of silence no clear answer had been given, Stevens might suggest a short break so that they could have a sidebar.

To his face they replied that it was, but a few days later they informed the company by e-mail that it was not. The Danish executive was aggrieved. "We'd already wasted weeks," he says. "Why didn't they tell us transparently during the meeting? We felt they had lied to us point-blank."

After hearing this story, I asked an Indonesian manager to explain what had happened. He told me that from an Indonesian perspective, it is rude to look someone you respect and like in the eye and say no to a request. "Instead we try to show 'no' with our body language or voice tone," he said. "Or perhaps we say, 'We will try our best.'" Signals like these are a way of saying "We would like to do what you want, but it is not possible." The interlocutor assumes that his counterpart will get the message and that both parties can then move on.

The problem can work the other way. The Indonesian manager went on to describe his experience negotiating with a French

In Japan, he said, it is common to iron out a lot of potential conflicts in one-on-one informal discussions before the formal group meeting, which is seen more as a place to put a stamp on decisions already made. This particular nugget came too late for that trip, but Stevens made sure the next time to enable informal discussions in advance. Thanks to her cultural bridge, she got the deal she had hoped for.

If your team has no obvious candidate for this role, look elsewhere in your company. But don't make the common mistake of thinking that someone who speaks the language and has a parent from the culture will necessarily make a good cultural bridge.

Consider this British manager of Korean origin: He looked Korean, had a Korean name, and spoke Korean with no accent, but he'd never lived or worked in Korea; his parents had moved to Britain as teenagers. His company asked him to help with an important negotiation in Korea, but once there, he quickly realized that his team would have been better off without him. Because he spoke the language so well, the Koreans assumed that he would behave like a Korean, so they took offense when he spoke to the wrong person in the room and when he confronted them too directly. As he observes, "If I hadn't looked or sounded Korean, they would have forgiven me for behaving badly."

company for the first time: "When I asked them if they could kindly do something, the word 'no' flew out of their mouths—and not just once but often more like a 'no-no-no-no,' which feels to us like we are being slapped repeatedly." He found out later that the French were actually happy to accede to his request; they had just wanted to debate it a bit before final agreement.

When you need to know whether your counterpart is willing to do something, but his answer to every question leaves you more confused than before, remember the fourth rule of cross-cultural negotiations: If possible, avoid posing a yes-or-no question. Rather than "Will you do this?" try "How long would it take you to get this done?" And when you do ask a yes-or-no question in Southeast Asia, Japan, or Korea (perhaps also in India or Latin America), engage all your senses and emotional antennae. Even if the response is affirmative, something may feel like no: an extra beat of silence, a strong sucking in of the breath, a muttered "I will try, but it will be diffi-cult." If so, the deal is probably not sealed. You may well have more negotiations in front of you.

5. Be Careful About Putting It in Writing

American managers learn early on to repeat key messages frequently and recap a meeting in writing. "Tell them what you're going to tell them, tell them, and then tell them what you've told them" is one of the first communication lessons taught in the United States. In Northern Europe, too, clarity and repetition are the basis of effective negotiation.

But this good practice can all too often sour during negotiations in Africa or Asia. A woman from Burundi who was working for a Dutch company says, "In my culture, if we have a discussion on the phone and come to a verbal agreement, that would be enough for me. If you get off the phone and send me a written recap of the dis-cussion, that would be a clear signal that you don't trust me." This, she says, repeatedly caused difficulty for her company's negotiators, who recapped each discussion in writing as a matter of both habit and principle.

The difference in approach can make it difficult to write a con-tract. Americans rely heavily on written contracts—more so than any other culture in the world. As soon as two parties have agreed on the price and details, long documents outlining what will happen if the deal is not kept, and requiring signatures, are exchanged. In the U.S. these contracts are legally binding and make it easy to do business with people we otherwise have no reason to trust.

But in countries where the legal system is traditionally less reli-able, and relationships carry more weight in business, written contracts are less frequent. In these countries they are often a com-mitment to do business but may not be legally binding. Therefore they're less detailed and less important. As one Nigerian manager explains, "If the moment we come to an agreement, you pull out the contract and hand me a pen, I start to worry. Do you think I won't follow through? Are you trying to trap me?"

In Nigeria and many other high-growth markets where the business environment is rapidly evolving, such as China and Indonesia, successful businesspeople must be much more flexible than is necessary (or desirable) in the West. In these cultures, a contract marks the beginning of a relationship, but it is understood that as the situation changes, the details of the agreement will also change.

Consider the experience of John Wagner, an American who had been working out a deal with a Chinese supplier. After several days of tough negotiations, his team and its legal department drafted a contract that the Chinese seemed happy to sign. But about six weeks later they reopened discussion on points that the Americans thought had been set in stone. Wagner observes, "I see now that we appeared irrationally inflexible to them. But at the time, we were hitting our heads against our desks." For the Americans, the contract had closed the negotiation phase, and implementation would follow. But for the Chinese, signing the contract was just one step in the dance.

So the fifth and final rule for negotiating internationally is to proceed cautiously with the contract. Ask your counterparts to draft the first version so that you can discern how much detail they are planning to commit to before you plunk down a 20-page document for them to sign. And be ready to revisit. When negotiating in emerging markets, remember that everything in these countries is dynamic, and no deal is ever really 100% final.

Finally, don't forget the universal rules: When you are negotiating a deal, you need to persuade and react, to convince and finesse, pushing your points while working carefully toward an agreement. In the heat of the discussion, what is spoken is important. But the trust you have built, the subtle messages you have understood, your ability to adapt your demeanor to the context at hand, will ultimately make the difference between success and failure—for Americans, for Chinese, for Brazilians, for everybody.

Originally published in December 2015. Reprint R1512E

The Limits of Empathy

by Adam Waytz

A FEW YEARS AGO, Ford Motor Company started asking its (mostly male) engineers to wear the Empathy Belly, a simulator that allows them to experience symptoms of pregnancy firsthand—the back pain, the bladder pressure, the 30 or so pounds of extra weight. They can even feel "movements" that mimic fetal kicking. The idea is to get them to understand the ergonomic challenges that pregnant women face when driving, such as limited reach, shifts in posture and center of gravity, and general bodily awkwardness.

It's unclear whether this has improved Ford's cars or increased customer satisfaction, but the engineers claim benefits from the experience. They're still using the belly; they're also simulating the foggy vision and stiff joints of elderly drivers with an "age suit." If nothing more, these exercises are certainly an attempt to "get the other person's point of view," which Henry Ford once famously said was the key to success.

Empathy is all the rage pretty much everywhere—not just at Ford, and not just on engineering and product development teams. It's at the heart of design thinking, and innovation more broadly defined. It's also touted as a critical leadership skill—one that helps you influence others in your organization, anticipate stakeholders' concerns, respond to social media followers, and even run better meetings.

But recent research (by me and many others) suggests that all this heat and light may be a bit too intense. Though empathy is essential to leading and managing others—without it, you'll make disastrous decisions and forfeit the benefits just described—failing to recognize its limits can impair individual and organizational performance.

Here are some of the biggest problems you can run into and recommendations for getting around them.

Problem #1: It's Exhausting

Like heavy-duty cognitive tasks, such as keeping multiple pieces of information in mind at once or avoiding distractions in a busy environment, empathy depletes our mental resources. So jobs that require constant empathy can lead to "compassion fatigue," an acute inability to empathize that's driven by stress, and burnout, a more gradual and chronic version of this phenomenon.

Health and human services professionals (doctors, nurses, social workers, corrections officers) are especially at risk, because empathy is central to their day-to-day jobs. In a study of hospice nurses, for example, the key predictors for compassion fatigue were psychological: anxiety, feelings of trauma, life demands, and what the researchers call excessive empathy, meaning the tendency to sacrifice one's own needs for others' (rather than simply "feeling" for people). Variables such as long hours and heavy caseloads also had an impact, but less than expected. And in a survey of Korean nurses, self-reported compassion fatigue strongly predicted their intentions to leave their jobs in the near future. Other studies of nurses show additional consequences of compassion fatigue, such as absenteeism and increased errors in administering medication.

People who work for charities and other nonprofits (think animal shelters) are similarly at risk. Voluntary turnover is exceedingly high, in part because of the empathically demanding nature of the work; low pay exacerbates the element of self-sacrifice. What's more, society's strict views of how nonprofits should operate mean they face a backlash when they act like businesses (for instance, investing in "overhead" to keep the organization running smoothly). They're

THE LIMITS OF EMPATHY

Idea in Brief

The Situation

We all know that empathy is essential to effective leadership, management, product development, marketing—pretty much any aspect of business that involves people. But it has its limits.

The Problems

Empathy taxes us mentally and emotionally, it's not an infinite resource, and it can even impair our ethical judgment. That's why if we demand too much of it from employees, performance will suffer.

The Solutions

You can take steps to prevent the ill effects and promote the good. For instance, have people focus on certain sets of stakeholders, help them meet others' needs in ways that also address their own, and give them empathy breaks so they can replenish their reserves.

expected to thrive through selfless outpourings of compassion from workers.

The demand for empathy is relentless in other sectors as well. Day after day, managers must motivate knowledge workers by understanding their experiences and perspectives and helping them find personal meaning in their work. Customer service professionals must continually quell the concerns of distressed callers. Empathy is exhausting in any setting or role in which it's a primary aspect of the job.

Problem #2: It's Zero-Sum

Empathy doesn't just drain energy and cognitive resources—it also depletes itself. The more empathy I devote to my spouse, the less I have left for my mother; the more I give to my mother, the less I can give my son. Both our desire to be empathic and the effort it requires are in limited supply, whether we're dealing with family and friends or customers and colleagues.

Consider this study: Researchers examined the trade-offs associated with empathic behaviors at work and at home by surveying 844 workers from various sectors, including hairstylists, firefighters, and telecom professionals. People who reported workplace behaviors such as taking "time to listen to coworkers' problems and worries" and helping "others who have heavy workloads" felt less capable of connecting with their families. They felt emotionally drained and burdened by work-related demands.

Sometimes the zero-sum problem leads to another type of trade-off: Empathy toward insiders—say, people on our teams or in our organizations—can limit our capacity to empathize with people outside our immediate circles. We naturally put more time and effort into understanding the needs of our close friends and colleagues. We simply find it easier to do, because we care more about them to begin with. This uneven investment creates a gap that's widened by our limited supply of empathy: As we use up most of what's available on insiders, our bonds with them get stronger, while our desire to connect with outsiders wanes.

Preferential empathy can antagonize those who see us as protecting our own (think about how people reacted when the Pope praised the Catholic Church's handling of sexual abuse). It can also, a bit more surprisingly, lead to insiders' aggression toward outsiders. For example, in a study I conducted with University of Chicago professor Nicholas Epley, we looked at how two sets of participants—those sitting with a friend (to prime empathic connection) and those sitting with a stranger—would treat a group of terrorists, an outgroup with particularly negative associations. After describing the terrorists, we asked how much participants endorsed statements portraying them as subhuman, how acceptable waterboarding them would be, and how much voltage of electric shock they would be willing to administer to them. Merely sitting in a room with a friend significantly increased people's willingness to torture and dehumanize.

Although this study represents an extreme case, the same principle holds for organizations. Compassion for one's own employees and colleagues sometimes produces aggressive responses toward others. More often, insiders are simply uninterested in empathizing with outsiders—but even that can cause people to neglect opportunities for constructive collaboration across functions or organizations.

Problem #3: It Can Erode Ethics

Finally, empathy can cause lapses in ethical judgment. We saw some of that in the study about terrorists. In many cases, though, the problem stems not from aggression toward outsiders but, rather, from extreme loyalty toward insiders. In making a focused effort to see and feel things the way people who are close to us do, we may take on their interests as our own. This can make us more willing to overlook transgressions or even behave badly ourselves.

Multiple studies in behavioral science and decision making show that people are more inclined to cheat when it serves another person. In various settings, with the benefits ranging from financial to reputational, people use this ostensible altruism to rationalize their dishonesty. It only gets worse when they empathize with another's plight or feel the pain of someone who is treated unfairly: In those cases, they're even more likely to lie, cheat, or steal to benefit that person.

In the workplace, empathy toward fellow employees can inhibit whistle-blowing—and when that happens, it seems scandals often follow. Just ask the police, the military, Penn State University, Citigroup, JPMorgan, and WorldCom. The kinds of problems that have plagued those organizations—brutality, sexual abuse, fraud—tend to be exposed by outsiders who don't identify closely with the perpetrators.

In my research with Liane Young and James Dungan of Boston College, we studied the effects of loyalty on people using Amazon's Mechanical Turk, an online marketplace where users earn money for completing tasks. At the beginning of the study, we asked some participants to write an essay about loyalty and others to write about fairness. Later in the study, they were each exposed to poor work by someone else. Those who had received the loyalty nudge were less willing to blow the whistle on a fellow user for inferior performance. This finding complements research showing that bribery is more common in countries that prize collectivism. The sense of group belonging and interdependence among members often leads people to tolerate the offense. It makes them feel less accountable for it, ffusing responsibility to the collective whole instead of assigning it to the individual.

In short, empathy for those within one's immediate circle can conflict with justice for all.

How to Rein In Excessive Empathy

These three problems may seem intractable, but as a manager you can do a number of things to mitigate them in your organization.

Split up the work

You might start by asking each employee to zero in on a certain set of stakeholders, rather than empathize with anyone and everyone. Some people can focus primarily on customers, for instance, and others on coworkers—think of it as creating task forces to meet different stakeholders' needs. This makes the work of developing relationships and gathering perspectives less consuming for individuals. You'll also accomplish more in the aggregate, by distributing "caring" responsibilities across your team or company. Although empathy is finite for any one person, it's less bounded when managed across employees.

Make it less of a sacrifice

Our mindsets can either intensify or lessen our susceptibility to empathy overload. For example, we exacerbate the zero-sum problem when we assume that our own interests and others' are fundamentally opposed. (This often happens in deal making, when parties with different positions on an issue get stuck because they're obsessed with the gap between them.) An adversarial mindset not only prevents us from understanding and responding to the other party but also makes us feel as though we've "lost" when we don't get our way. We can avoid burnout by seeking integrative solutions that serve both sides' interests.

Take this example: A salary negotiation between a hiring manager and a promising candidate will become a tug-of-war contest if they have different numbers in mind and fixate on the money alone.

THE LIMITS OF EMPATHY

But let's suppose that the candidate actually cares more about job security, and the manager is keenly interested in avoiding turnover. Building security into the contract would be a win-win: an empathic act by the manager that wouldn't drain his empathy reserves the way making a concession on salary would, because keeping new hires around is in line with his own desires.

There's only so much empathy to go around, but it's possible to achieve economies of sorts. By asking questions instead of letting assumptions go unchecked, you can bring such solutions to the surface.

Give people breaks

As a management and organizations professor, I cringe when students refer to my department's coursework—on leadership, teams, and negotiation—as "soft skills." Understanding and responding to the needs, interests, and desires of other human beings involves some of the *hardest* work of all. Despite claims that empathy comes naturally, it takes arduous mental effort to get into another person's mind—and then to respond with compassion rather than indifference.

We all know that people need periodic relief from technical and analytical work and from rote jobs like data entry. The same is true of empathy. Look for ways to give employees breaks. It's not sufficient to encourage self-directed projects that also benefit the company (and often result in more work), as Google did with its 20% time policy. Encourage individuals to take time to focus on their interests alone. Recent research finds that people who take lots of self-focused breaks subsequently report feeling more empathy for others. That might seem counterintuitive, but when people feel restored, they're better able to perform the demanding tasks of figuring out and responding to what others need.

How do you give people respite from thinking and caring about others? Some companies are purchasing isolation chambers like Orrb Technologies' wellness and learning pods so that people can literally put themselves in a bubble to relax, meditate, or do whatever else helps them recharge. McLaren, for example, uses the pods to train F1 supercar drivers to focus. Other companies, such as electrical parts distributor Van Meter, are relying on much simpler interventions like shutting off employee e-mail accounts when workers go on vacation to allow them to concentrate on themselves without interruption.

Despite its limitations, empathy is essential at work. So managers should make sure employees are investing it wisely.

When trying to empathize, it's generally better to talk with people about their experiences than to imagine how they might be feeling, as Nicholas Epley suggests in his book *Mindwise*. A recent study bears this out. Participants were asked how capable they thought blind people were of working and living independently. But before answering the question, some were asked to complete difficult physical tasks while wearing a blindfold. Those who had done the blindness simulation judged blind people to be much less capable. That's because the exercise led them to ask "What would it be like if *I* were blind?" (the answer: very difficult!) rather than "What is it like for *a blind person* to be blind?" This finding speaks to why Ford's use of the Empathy Belly, while well-intentioned, may be misguided: After wearing it, engineers may overestimate or misidentify the difficulties faced by drivers who actually are pregnant.

Talking to people—asking them how they feel, what they want, and what they think—may seem simplistic, but it's more accurate. It's also less taxing to employees and their organizations, because it involves collecting real information instead of endlessly speculating. It's a smarter way to empathize.

Originally published in January–February 2016. Reprint R1601D

People Before Strategy

A New Role for the CHRO. *by Ram Charan, Dominic Barton, and Dennis Carey*

CEOS KNOW THAT they depend on their company's human resources to achieve success. Businesses don't create value; people do. But if you peel back the layers at the vast majority of companies, you find CEOs who are distanced from and often dissatisfied with their chief human resources officers (CHROs) and the HR function in general. Research by McKinsey and the Conference Board consistently finds that CEOs worldwide see human capital as a top challenge, and they rank HR as only the eighth or ninth most important function in a company. That has to change.

It's time for HR to make the same leap that the finance function has made in recent decades and become a true partner to the CEO. Just as the CFO helps the CEO lead the business by raising and allocating financial resources, the CHRO should help the CEO by building and assigning talent, especially key people, and working to unleash the organization's energy. Managing human capital must be accorded the same priority that managing financial capital came to have in the 1980s, when the era of the "super CFO" and serious competitive restructuring began.

CEOs might complain that their CHROs are too bogged down in administrative tasks or that they don't understand the business. But let's be clear: It is up to the CEO to elevate HR and to bridge any gaps that prevent the CHRO from becoming a strategic partner. After all, it was CEOs who boosted the finance function beyond simple accounting. They were also responsible for creating the marketing function from what had been strictly sales.

Elevating HR requires totally redefining the work content of the chief human resources officer—in essence, forging a new contract with this leader—and adopting a new mechanism we call the G3—a core group comprising the CEO, the CFO, and the CHRO. The result will be a CHRO who is as much a value adder as the CFO. Rather than being seen as a supporting player brought in to implement decisions that have already been made, the CHRO will have a central part in corporate decision making and will be properly prepared for that role.

These changes will drive important shifts in career paths for HR executives—and for other leaders across the company. Moreover, the business will benefit from better management of not just its financial resources but also its human ones. We say this with confidence, based on our experience with companies such as General Electric, BlackRock, Tata Communications, and Marsh, all of which act on their commitment to the people side of their businesses.

The CEO's New Contract with the CHRO

A CFO's job is partly defined by the investment community, the board, outside auditors, and regulators. Not so for the CHRO role—that's defined solely by the CEO. The chief executive must have a clear view of the tremendous contribution the CHRO could be making and spell out those expectations in clear, specific language. Putting things in writing ensures that the CEO and CHRO have a shared understanding of appropriate actions and desirable outputs.

To start redefining the job, the CEO should confer with his or her team and key board members, particularly the board's compensation committee (more aptly called the talent and compensation committee), and ask what they expect in an ideal CHRO. Beyond handling the usual HR responsibilities—overseeing employee satisfaction,

Idea in Brief

The Problem

CEOs consistently rank human capital as a top challenge, but they typically undervalue their chief human resources officer and view HR as less important than other functions.

The Solution

The chief human resources officer must become a true strategic partner to the CEO.

The Approach

The CEO must rewrite the CHRO's job description and create a core decision-making body comprising the CEO, CFO, and CHRO.

---

workforce engagement, benefits and compensation, diversity, and the like—what should an exemplary CHRO do?

Here are three activities we think are critical: predicting outcomes, diagnosing problems, and prescribing actions on the people side that will add value to the business. Some of these things may seem like the usual charter for a CHRO, but they are largely missing in practice, to the disappointment of most CEOs.

Predicting outcomes

CEOs and CFOs normally put together a three-year plan and a one-year budget. The CHRO should be able to assess the chances of meeting the business goals using his knowledge of the people side. How likely is it, for example, that a key group or leader will make timely changes in tune with rapid shifts in the external environment, or that team members will be able to coordinate their efforts? CHROs should raise such questions and offer their views.

Because a company's performance depends largely on the fit between people and jobs, the CHRO can be of enormous help by crystallizing what a particular job requires and realistically assessing whether the assigned person meets those requirements. Jobs that are high leverage require extra attention. Many HR processes tend to treat all employees the same way, but in our observation, 2% of the people in a business drive 98% of the impact. Although coaching can be helpful, particularly when it focuses on one or two things that are preventing individuals from reaching their potential, it has its limits. Nothing overcomes a poor fit. A wide gap between a leader's talents and the job requirements creates problems for the leader, her boss, her peers, and her reports. So before severe damage is done, the CHRO should take the initiative to identify gaps in behavior or skills, especially among those 2% and as job requirements change.

The CHRO, with the CFO, should also consider whether the key performance indicators, talent assignments, and budgets are the right ones to deliver desired outcomes. If necessary, the pair should develop new metrics. Financial information is the most common basis for incentivizing and assessing performance, because it is easy to measure, but the CHRO can propose alternatives. People should be paid according to how much value they contribute to the company—some combination of the importance of the job and how they handle it. Finance and HR should work together to define ahead of time the value that is expected, using qualitative as well as quantitative factors. Imagine the leaders of those functions discussing a business unit manager and triangulating with the CEO and the group executive to better understand what the manager needs to do to outperform the competition in the heat of battle. For example, to move faster into digitization, will he have to reconstitute the team or reallocate funds? Predicting success means weighing how well-attuned the manager is to outside pressures and opportunities, how resilient he would be if the economy went south, and how quickly he could scale up into digitization. The specific metrics would be designed accordingly.

As another example, a top marketing manager might have to build capability for using predictive data in advertising. The CFO and CHRO should recognize that if the manager fails to steep herself in the fundamentals of data analytics and is slow to hire people with that expertise, new competitors could come in and destroy value for the company. Metrics should reflect how quickly the marketing head acts to reorient her department. One set of metrics would focus on the recruiting plan: What steps must the marketing manager take by when? These become milestones to be met at particular points in time. Another set of metrics might focus on budget allocations: Once the new people are hired and assimilated, is the manager reallocating the marketing budget? And is that money in fact helping to increase revenue, margins, market share in selected segments, or brand recognition? Such improvements are measurable, though with a time lag.

The CHRO should also be able to make meaningful predictions about the competition. Just as every army general learns about his counterpart on the enemy side, the CHRO should be armed with information about competitors and how their key decision makers and executors stack up against those at the CHRO's organization. Predictions should include the likely impact of any changes related to human resources at rival companies—such as modifications to their incentive systems, an increase in turnover, or new expertise they are hiring—and what those changes might signify about their market moves. In 2014, for instance, Apple began to hire medical technology people—an early warning sign that it might make a heavy push to use its watch and perhaps other Apple devices for medical purposes. Such activity could have implications for a health care business, a medical device manufacturer, or a clinic. Similarly, a competitor's organizational restructuring and reassignment of leaders might indicate a sharper focus on product lines that could give your company a tougher run.

Intelligence about competitors is often available through headhunters, the press, employees hired from other companies, suppliers, or customers' customers. Even anecdotal information, such as "The marketing VP is a numbers guy, not a people guy," or "She's a cost cutter and can't grow the business," or "The head of their new division comes from a high-growth company," can improve the power of prediction. For example, Motorola might have been able to anticipate the iPhone if the company's CHRO had alerted the CEO when Apple began trying to recruit Motorola's technical people.

The CHRO should make comparisons unit by unit, team by team, and leader by leader, looking not only at established competitors but also at nontraditional ones that could enter the market. Is the person who was promoted to run hair care at X company more experienced and higher-energy than our new division head? Does the development team in charge of wireless sensors at Y company collaborate better than we do? The answers to such questions will help predict outcomes that will show up as numbers on a financial statement sometime in the future.

Diagnosing problems

The CHRO is in a position to pinpoint precisely why an organization might not be performing well or meeting its goals. CEOs must learn to seek such analysis from their CHROs instead of defaulting to consultants.

The CHRO should work with the CEO and CFO to examine the causes of misses, because most problems are people problems. The idea is to look beyond obvious external factors, such as falling interest rates or shifting currency valuations, and to link the numbers with insights into the company's social system—how people work together. A correct diagnosis will suggest the right remedy and avoid any knee-jerk replacements of people who made good decisions but were dealt a bad hand.

If the economy slumped and performance lagged compared to the previous year, the question should be, How did the leader react? Did he get caught like a deer in the headlights or go on the offensive? How fast did he move, relative to the competition and the external change? This is where the CHRO can help make the critical distinction between a leader's misstep and any fundamental unsuitability for the job. Here too the CHRO will learn new things about the leader, such as how resilient he is—information that will be useful in considering future assignments.

But focusing on individual leaders is only half the equation. The CHRO should also be expert at diagnosing how the various parts of the social system are working, systematically looking for activities that are causing bottlenecks or unnecessary friction. When one CEO was reviewing the numbers for an important product line, he saw a decline in market share and profits for the third year in a row. The medical diagnostic product that the group was counting on to reverse the trend was still not ready to launch. As he and his CHRO dug in, they discovered that the marketing team in Milwaukee and the R&D team in France had not agreed on the specifications. On the spot, they arranged a series of face-to-face meetings to resolve the disconnect.

There is great value in having the CHRO diagnose problems and put issues on the table, but such openness is often missing. Behaviors such as withholding information, failing to express disagreement but refusing to take action, and undermining peers often go unnoticed. Some CEOs look the other way rather than tackle conflicts among their direct reports, draining energy and making the whole organization indecisive. Take, for example, problems that arise when collaboration across silos doesn't happen. In such situations, no amount of cost cutting, budget shifting, or admonition will stem the deterioration. Thus CHROs who bring dysfunctional relationships to the surface are worth their weight in gold.

At the same time, the CHRO should watch for employees who are energy creators and develop them. Whether or not they are directly charged with producing results, these are the people who get to the heart of issues, reframe ideas, create informal bonds that encourage collaboration, and in general make the organization healthier and more productive. They may be the hidden power behind the group's value creation.

Prescribing actions to add value

Agile companies know they must move capital to where the opportunities are and not succumb to the all-too-typical imperatives of budgeting inertia ("You get the same funding as last year, plus or minus 5%"). When McKinsey looked at capital allocation patterns in more than 1,600 U.S. companies over 15 years, it found that aggressive reallocators—companies that shifted more than 56% of capital across businesses during that time—had 30% higher total shareholder returns than companies that shifted far less.

Companies should be similarly flexible with their human capital, and CHROs should be prepared to recommend actions that will unlock or create value. These might include recognizing someone's hidden talent and adding that individual to the list of high potentials, moving someone from one position to another to ignite growth in a new market, or bringing in someone from the outside to develop capability in a new technology. Although capital reallocation is important, the reassignment of people along with capital reallocation is what really boosts companies.

Responding to the external environment today sometimes requires leaders with capabilities that weren't previously cultivated, such as knowledge of algorithms, or psychological comfort with digitization and rapid change. The company might have such talent buried at low levels. To have impact, those individuals might need to be lifted three organizational levels at once rather than moved incrementally up existing career ladders. The CHRO should be searching for people who could be future value creators and then thinking imaginatively about how to release their talent. Judging people must be a special skill of the CHRO, just as the CFO has a knack for making inferences from numbers.

Dow Chemical found that aggressively hiring entrepreneurial millennials was the fastest way to create more "short-cycle innovation" alongside the company's traditional long-cycle R&D processes. The share of employees under age 30 went from 9% in 2004 to 15% in 2014. To benefit from this new talent, the company also revamped its career paths to move the 20- and 30-somethings into bigger jobs relatively quickly, and it invited them to global leadership meetings relatively early.

Another way to unlock value is to recommend mechanisms to help an individual bridge a gap or enhance her capacity. These might include moving her to a different job, establishing a council to advise her, or assigning someone to help shore up a particular skill. For example, to build the technology expertise of the small start-ups he funded, the famed venture capitalist John Doerr used his huge relationship network to connect the people running those businesses with top scientists at Bell Labs. In the same vein, CHROs could make better use of their networks with other CHROs to connect people with others who could build their capacity.

The CHRO might also recommend splitting a division into subgroups to unleash growth and develop more P&L leaders. He might suggest particular skills to look for when hiring a leader to run a country unit or big division. Other prescriptions might focus on improving the social engine—the quality of relationships, the level of trust and collaboration, and decisiveness. The CHRO could, for instance, work with business divisions to conduct reviews once a month rather than annually, because reducing the time lag between actions and feedback increases motivation and improves operations.

What not to do
In addition to spelling out clearly what is expected in the way of making predictions, diagnosing problems, and prescribing beneficial actions, the CHRO's new contract should define what she is *not* required to do. This helps provide focus and free time so that she can engage at a higher level. For example, the transactional and administrative work of HR, including managing benefits, could be cordoned off and reassigned, as some companies have begun to do. One option is to give those responsibilities to the CFO. At Netflix, traditional HR processes and routines are organized under the finance function, while HR serves only as a talent scout and coach. Another model we see emerging is to create a shared service function that combines the back-office activities of HR, finance, and IT. This function may or may not report to the CFO.

Compensation has traditionally been the purview of CHROs, but it may be hard for them to appreciate the specific issues business leaders face, just as it is hard for the CFO to understand the nuances of the social engine. Because compensation has such an enormous impact on behavior and on the speed and agility of the corporation, the best solution is for the CEO and CFO to also get involved. While the CHRO can be the lead dog, compensation decisions should be made jointly by the three—and, given the increasingly active role of institutional investors, with the board's engagement.

The CHRO's fit
With a new contract in hand, the chief executive should assess how well the CHRO meets the job specifications now and where he

needs to be in three years. Most CHROs have come up through the HR pipeline. While some have had line jobs, most have not; Korn Ferry research indicates that only 40 of the CHROs at *Fortune* 100 companies had significant work experience outside HR before they came to lead that function. This might leave a gap in terms of predicting, diagnosing, and prescribing actions that will improve business performance. However, inclusion in broader discussions will expand a CHRO's understanding of the business. CEOs should give their CHRO a chance to grow into the newly defined role, and they should assess progress quarter by quarter.

Measuring the performance of the CHRO has long been problematic. HR leaders are usually judged on accomplishments such as installing a new process under budget, recruiting a targeted number of people from the right places, or improving retention or employee engagement. Yet such efforts are not directly tied to value creation. In keeping with recasting HR as a value creator rather than a cost center, performance should be measured by outputs that are more closely linked to revenue, profit margin, brand recognition, or market share. And the closer the linkage, the better.

A CHRO can add value by, for example, moving a key person from one boss to another and improving his performance; arranging for coaching that strengthens a crucial skill; bringing a person from the outside into a pivotal position; putting two or three people together to create a new business or initiative to grow the top or bottom line; reassigning a division manager because she will not be able to meet the challenge two years out; or discovering and smoothing friction where collaboration is required. Such actions are observable, verifiable, and closely related to the company's performance and numbers.

Here's a case in point: When a promising young leader was put in charge of three divisions of a large company, replacing an executive vice president with long tenure, the divisions took off. The new EVP, who was growth-oriented and digitally savvy, seized on commonalities among the three businesses in technology and production and nearly halved the product development cycle time. In three years the divisions overtook the competition to become number one.

Creating a G3

To make the CHRO a true partner, the CEO should create a triumvirate at the top of the corporation that includes both the CFO and the CHRO. Forming such a team is the single best way to link financial numbers with the people who produce them. It also signals to the organization that you are lifting HR into the inner sanctum and that the CHRO's contribution will be analogous to the CFO's. Although some companies may want the CHRO to be part of an expanded group that includes, say, a chief technology officer or chief risk officer, the G3, as we call it, is the core group that should steer the company, and it should meet apart from everyone else. The G3 will shape the destiny of the business by looking forward and at the big picture while others bury their heads in operations, and it will ensure that the company stays on the rails by homing in on any problems in execution. It is the G3 that makes the connection between the organization and business results.

At Marsh, a global leader in insurance brokerage and risk management, CEO Peter Zaffino often has one-on-one discussions with his CFO, Courtney Leimkuhler, and his CHRO, Mary Anne Elliott. In April 2015 he held a meeting with both of them to assess the alignment of the organization with desired business outcomes. The G3 began this meeting by selecting a business in the portfolio and drawing a vertical line down the middle of a blank page on a flip chart. The right side was for the business performance (Leimkuhler's expertise); the left side for organizational design issues (Elliott's expertise). A horizontal line created boxes for the answers to two simple questions: What is going well? What is not going well?

"Peter could have filled in the entire two-by-two chart on his own," Elliott says, "but doing it together really added value." Zaffino adds, "The whole meeting took about 15 minutes. We found the exercise to be very worthwhile. We already run the business with disciplined processes. We conduct deep dives into the organization's financial performance through quarterly operational reviews, and we conduct quarterly talent reviews, where we focus on the human capital side. So you might not think we'd want to introduce another process to evaluate how we are managing the business. But this G3 process provided us with a terrific lens into the business without adding bureaucracy."

Working together to synthesize disparate data points into one flip chart helped the team identify items on the organizational side that would predict business performance in the next four to eight quarters. Significant value came from the dialogue as connections emerged naturally. Zaffino says, "We constantly drill down deep to understand why a business is performing the way it is. In those instances, we are drilling vertically, not horizontally, when there could be some items identified on the organizational side that are actually driving the performance." Zaffino cited the implementation of a new sales plan, which HR was working on, as one example. His concern was making sure business results were aligned with remuneration "so we didn't have sales compensation becoming disconnected from the overall financial result of the business," he explains. "We also didn't want to drive top-line growth without knowing how to invest back in the business and increase profitability." The CHRO was thinking it through from her perspective: Is this sales plan motivating the right behaviors so that it moves business performance to the "going well" category?

Seeing the interconnections also helped the trio identify what mattered most. "It's easy enough to list everything we want to do better," Leimkuhler says, "but it's hard to know where to start. When you understand which things on the organizational side are really advancing business performance, it makes it easier to prioritize." For example, managing the transition of regional business leaders was a big issue for HR—one that, because of its difficulty, would have been easy to push off. Seeing the extent to which inaction could be holding back business performance created a greater sense of urgency.

"In the HR world, we talk about understanding and integrating with the business," Elliott notes. "G3 meetings are a pragmatic activity. When you're sitting with the CEO and CFO, there's no place for academic HR. It's all about understanding what the organization needs to do to drive business performance and how to align those key variables."

"There's something to be said for peeling off into a smaller group," Leimkuhler adds. "It would be unwieldy to have this discussion with the full executive committee, which at Marsh consists of 10 executives. In any case, it's not one or the other; it's additive." Says Zaffino, "This was a streamlined way to get a holistic view of the business. Each of us left the first G3 meeting feeling comfortable that the organization and the business were aligned and that we have a very good handle on the business."

Vinod Kumar, CEO of Tata Communications, also uses an informal G3 mechanism. Kumar's company supplies communication, computing, and collaboration infrastructure to large global companies, including many telephone and mobile operators. In 2012 there were price drops of 15% to 20%, and disruptive technologies were par for the course. To keep pace, Tata Communications had to transform its business very quickly, which meant building critical new capabilities by hiring from the outside, at least in the short term—an effort that would hardly help the company deal with rising costs. Something had to give, and Kumar enlisted then-CFO Sanjay Baweja and CHRO Aadesh Goyal to help chart a path forward while taking into account both financial and talent considerations.

Frequent discussions among the G3 led to a consensus: Tata Communications would restructure roles that had become redundant or were out of sync with the company's new direction, and it would move jobs to the right geographical locations. These actions would reduce staffing costs by 7%. The company would use the savings to build the necessary capabilities, mainly by making new hires, especially in sales, marketing, and technology.

The G3 next went to work on changes that would occur over a longer time. Tata Communications launched a companywide program in late 2013 aimed at continuously improving productivity. The initial objective was to reduce the cost base by $100 million, but the overall intention was to seed a new culture. The G3 began by creating a cross-functional team that employees joined part-time. Ultimately more than 500 people participated, working on ideas in

50 categories and achieving even more cost reductions than originally targeted. In short, the project was a big success, and it continues to produce results.

Dialogue—both institutionalized and informal—between the CHRO, the CFO, and the CEO is now a way of life at Tata Communications. In time, as CHRO Goyal's grasp of the business became evident, Kumar made a bold move: He gave Goyal the additional responsibility of managing one of the company's high-growth subsidiaries and made him part of the Innovation Council, which identifies opportunities to invest in and incubate new businesses.

Regular G3 Meetings

If a G3 is to be effective, the CEO has to ensure that the triumvirate meets on a regular basis.

Weekly temperature taking

The CEO, CFO, and CHRO should get together once a week to discuss any early warning signals they are picking up internally or externally about the condition of the social engine. Each of them will see things through a different lens, and pooling their thoughts will yield a more accurate picture. The three don't have to be together physically—they can arrange a conference call or video chat—but meeting frequently is important. After about six weeks, and with discipline, such sessions could be finished in 15 to 20 minutes.

The CEO has to set the tone for these reviews, ensuring that the discussion is balanced and that intellectual honesty and integrity are absolute. It's a given that both the CFO and the CHRO must be politically neutral to build trust, and they must never sacrifice their integrity to be the CEO's henchmen. They must be willing to speak up and tell it like it is. Over time, each G3 member will have a better understanding of the others' cognitive lenses, discussions will be more fluid, and all three will learn a lot about the intricacies of the business. They will also become more comfortable correcting one another's biases, more skilled at reading people, and more likely to get the right people in the right jobs.

Looking forward monthly

The G3 should spend a couple of hours every month looking four and eight quarters ahead with these questions in mind: What people issues would prevent us from meeting our goals? Is there a problem with an individual? With collaboration? Is a senior team member unable to see how the competition is moving? Is somebody likely to leave us?

Companies do operational reviews, which are backward-looking, at least quarterly. The objective here is to be predictive and diagnostic, looking forward not just at the numbers but also at the people side, because most failures and missed opportunities are people-related. There may be organizational issues, energy drains, or conflicts among silos, particularly in the top two layers. Conflicts are inherent in matrix organizations; the G3 needs to know where they exist, whether they could affect progress on a new initiative, and how the leaders in charge are handling them. Probing such matters is not micromanagement or a witch hunt. It's a means of finding the real causes of both good and poor performance and taking corrective action promptly or preemptively.

Planning three years out

It is common practice to plan where the company needs to be in three years and to decide what new projects to fund and where to invest capital. Often missing from that process is exploration of the people questions: Will we have employees with the right skills, training, and temperament to achieve the targets? Will our people have the flexibility to adapt to changing circumstances? In most strategic planning, there is zero consideration of the critical players in the organization—or those working for competitors.

Discussion of people should come before discussion of strategy. (This is a practice that General Electric is known for.) What are employees' capabilities, what help might they need, and are they the very best? The CEO and the CHRO of one company decided that for every high-leverage position that opened, they should have five candidates—three from inside, two from outside. Talent should always be viewed in a broad context. Consider who is excelling, being let go, or being lured away, along with any other information that could affect your competitiveness or your rivals'.

New HR Leadership Channels

Some CEOs might be holding back on elevating their CHROs because they lack confidence in the HR leader's business judgment and people acumen. There's a fear that HR chiefs aren't prepared to discuss issues beyond hiring, firing, payroll, benefits, and the like. That reservation must be met head-on by providing rich opportunities for CHROs to learn. Give them more exposure to the business side through meetings of the G3, and provide some coaching. If knowledge or skills gaps persist, ask the CHRO how she might fill them. Some CHROs will rise to the occasion. Others won't measure up, and the supply of suitable replacements might be scarce at first. (The same issue applied in the 1980s to finding the right CFO types from the ranks of accounting.)

An enduring solution is to create new career paths for HR leaders to cultivate business smarts and for business leaders to cultivate people smarts. Every entry-level leader, whether in HR or some other job, should get rigorous training in judging, recruiting, and coaching people. And those who begin their careers in HR leadership should go through rigorous training in business analysis, along the lines of what McKinsey requires for all its new recruits. There should be no straight-line leadership promotions up the functional HR silo. Aspiring CHROs should have line jobs along the way, where they have to manage people and budgets.

All leaders headed for top jobs should alternate between positions in HR and in the rest of the business. Make it a requirement for people in the top three layers of the company to have successfully worked as an HR leader, and the function will soon become a talent magnet. Be sure that it isn't just ticket punching. Those who have no feel for the people side are unlikely to succeed for long in high-level jobs.

The Transition to the New HR

Any CEO who is sold on the idea that people are the ultimate source of sustainable competitive differentiation must take the rejuvenation and elevation of the HR function very seriously. Creating a mechanism that knits the CFO and the CHRO together will improve the business and expand the CEO's personal capability. It won't happen overnight—three years seems to us the minimum time required to achieve a shift of this magnitude. Stating the new expectations for the CHRO and the human resources function is a good place to begin. Creating ways to blend business and people acumen should follow. And redesigning career tracks and talent reviews will take the company further still. But none of this will happen unless the CEO personally embraces the challenge, makes a three-year commitment, and starts executing.

Originally published in July–August 2015. Reprint R1507D

Beyond Automation

by Thomas H. Davenport and Julia Kirby

AFTER HEARING OF a recent Oxford University study on advancing automation and its potential to displace workers, Yuh-Mei Hutt, of Tallahassee, Florida, wrote, "The idea that half of today's jobs may vanish has changed my view of my children's future." Hutt was reacting not only as a mother; she heads a business and occasionally blogs about emerging technologies. Familiar as she is with the upside of computerization, the downside looms large. "How will they compete against AI?" she asked. "How will they compete against a much older and experienced workforce vying for even fewer positions?"

Suddenly, it seems, people in all walks of life are becoming very concerned about advancing automation. And they should be: Unless we find as many tasks to give humans as we find to take away from them, all the social and psychological ills of joblessness will grow, from economic recession to youth unemployment to individual crises of identity. That's especially true now that automation is coming to knowledge work, in the form of artificial intelligence (see the exhibit "Three eras of automation"). Knowledge work—which we'll define loosely as work that is more mental than manual, involves consequential decision making, and has traditionally required a college education—accounts for a large proportion of jobs in today's mature economies. It is the high ground to which humanity has retreated as machines have taken over less cognitively challenging work. But in the very foreseeable future, as the Gartner analyst Nigel Rayner says, "many of the things executives do today will be automated."

What if we were to reframe the situation? What if, rather than asking the traditional question—What tasks currently performed by humans will soon be done more cheaply and rapidly by machines?—we ask a new one: What new feats might people achieve if they had better thinking machines to assist them? Instead of seeing work as a zero-sum game with machines taking an ever greater share, we might see growing possibilities for employment. We could reframe the threat of *automation* as an opportunity for *augmentation.*

The two of us have been looking at cases in which knowledge workers collaborate with machines to do things that neither could do well on their own. And as automation makes greater incursions into their workplaces, these people respond with a surprisingly broad repertoire of moves. Conventional wisdom is that as machines threaten their livelihood, humans must invest in ever higher levels of formal education to keep ahead. In truth, as we will discuss below, smart people are taking five approaches to making their peace with smart machines.

What Is Augmentation?

David Autor, an economist at MIT who closely tracks the effects of automation on labor markets, recently complained that "journalists and expert commentators overstate the extent of machine substitution for human labor and ignore the strong complementarities that increase productivity, raise earnings, and augment demand for skilled labor." He pointed to the immense challenge of applying machines to any tasks that call for flexibility, judgment, or common sense, and then pushed his point further. "Tasks that cannot be substituted by computerization are generally complemented by it," he wrote. "This point is as fundamental as it is overlooked."

A search for the complementarities to which Autor was referring is at the heart of what we call an augmentation strategy. It stands in stark contrast to the automation strategies that efficiency-minded enterprises have pursued in the past. Automation starts with a baseline of what people do in a given job and subtracts from that. It deploys computers to chip away at the tasks humans perform as soon as those tasks can be codified. Aiming for increased

Idea in Brief

The Threat

Automation has traditionally displaced workers, forcing them onto higher ground that machines have not yet claimed. Today, as artificial intelligence encroaches on knowledge work, it can be hard to see how humans will remain employed in large numbers.

The Reframing

The outlook is grim if computers continue to chip away relentlessly at the tasks currently performed by well-educated people. But if we reframe the use of machines as *augmentation*, human work can flourish and accomplish what was never before possible.

Five Steps

Some knowledge workers will *step up* to even higher levels of cognition; others will *step aside* and draw on forms of intelligence that machines lack. Some will *step in*, monitoring and adjusting computers' decision making; others will *step narrowly* into highly specialized realms of expertise. Inevitably, some will *step forward* by creating next-generation machines and finding new ways for them to augment human strengths.

automation promises cost savings but limits us to thinking within the parameters of work that is being accomplished today.

Augmentation, in contrast, means starting with what humans do today and figuring out how that work could be deepened rather than diminished by a greater use of machines. Some thoughtful knowledge workers see this clearly. Camille Nicita, for example, is the CEO of Gongos, a company in metropolitan Detroit that helps clients gain consumer insights—a line of work that some would say is under threat as big data reveals all about buying behavior. Nicita concedes that sophisticated decision analytics based on large data sets will uncover new and important insights. But, she says, that will give her people the opportunity to go deeper and offer clients "context, humanization, and the 'why' behind big data." Her shop will increasingly "go beyond analysis and translate that data in a way that informs business decisions through synthesis and the power of great narrative." Fortunately, computers aren't very good at that sort of thing.

Intelligent machines, Nicita thinks—and this is the core belief of an augmentation strategy—do not usher people out the door,

Three eras of automation

If this wave of automation seems scarier than previous ones, it's for good reason. As machines encroach on decision making, it's hard to see the higher ground to which humans might move.

Era one	Era two	Era three
Machines take away the *dirty and dangerous*—industrial equipment, from looms to the cotton gin, relieves humans of onerous manual labor.	Machines take away the *dull*—automated interfaces, from airline kiosks to call centers, relieve humans of routine service transactions and clerical chores.	Machines take away *decisions*—intelligent systems, from airfare pricing to IBM's Watson, make better choices than humans, reliably and fast.
19th century	20th century	21st century

→

much less relegate them to doing the bidding of robot overlords. In some cases these machines will allow us to take on tasks that are superior—more sophisticated, more fulfilling, better suited to our strengths—to anything we have given up. In other cases the tasks will simply be different from anything computers can do well. In almost all situations, however, they will be less codified and structured; otherwise computers would already have taken them over.

We propose a change in mindset, on the part of both workers and providers of work, that will lead to different outcomes—a change from pursuing automation to promoting augmentation. This seemingly simple terminological shift will have deep implications for how organizations are managed and how individuals strive to succeed. Knowledge workers will come to see smart machines as partners and collaborators in creative problem solving.

This new mindset could change the future.

Five Steps to Consider

Let's assume that computers are going to make their mark in your line of work. Indeed, let's posit that software will soon perform most of the cognitive heavy lifting you do in your job and, as far as the essential day-to-day operation of the enterprise is concerned, make decisions as good as (probably better than) those made by 90% of the people who currently hold it. What should your strategy be to remain gainfully employed? From an augmentation perspective, people might renegotiate their relationship to machines and realign their contributions in five ways.

Step up

Your best strategy may be to head for still higher intellectual ground. There will always be jobs for people who are capable of more big-picture thinking and a higher level of abstraction than computers are. In essence this is the same advice that has always been offered and taken as automation has encroached on human work: Let the machine do the things that are beneath you, and take the opportunity to engage with higher-order concerns.

Niven Narain, a cancer researcher, provides a great example. In 2005 he cofounded Berg, a start-up in Framingham, Massachusetts, to apply artificial intelligence to the discovery of new drugs. Berg's facility has high-throughput mass spectrometers that run around the clock and produce trillions of data points from their analysis of blood and tissue, along with powerful computers that look for patterns suggesting that certain molecules could be effective. "The last thing you want to do now," Narain told a reporter in March 2015, "is have a hundred biochemists . . . going through this data and saying, 'Oh, I kind of like this one over here.'" But he also employs a hundred biochemists. Their objective is not to crunch all those numbers and produce a hypothesis about a certain molecule's potential. Rather, they pick up at the point where the math leaves off, the machine has produced a hypothesis, and the investigation of its viability begins.

Narain stepped up by seeing an opportunity to develop drugs in a new way. That takes lots of experience, insight, and the ability to understand quickly how the world is changing. Likewise, one interpretation of the success of today's ultrarich Wall Street investment bankers and hedge fund titans is that they have stepped up above automated trading and portfolio management systems.

If stepping up is your chosen approach, you will probably need a long education. A master's degree or a doctorate will serve you well as a job applicant. Once inside an organization, your objective must be to stay broadly informed and creative enough to be part of its ongoing innovation and strategy efforts. Ideally you'll aspire to a senior management role and thus seize the opportunities you identify. Listen to Barney Harford, the CEO of Orbitz—a business that has done more than most to eliminate knowledge worker jobs. To hire for the tasks he still requires people to do, Harford looks for "T-shaped" individuals. Orbitz needs "people who can go really deep in their particular area of expertise," he says, "and also go really broad and have that kind of curiosity about the overall organization and how their particular piece of the pie fits into it." That's good guidance for any knowledge worker who wants to step up: Start thinking more synthetically—in the old sense of that term. Find ways to rely on machines to do your intellectual spadework, without losing knowledge of how they do it. Harford has done that by applying "machine learning" to the generation of algorithms that match customers with the travel experiences they desire.

Step aside

Stepping up may be an option for only a small minority of the labor force. But a lot of brain work is equally valuable and also cannot be codified. Stepping aside means using mental strengths that aren't about purely rational cognition but draw on what the psychologist Howard Gardner has called our "multiple intelligences." You might focus on the "interpersonal" and "intrapersonal" intelligences—knowing how to work well with other people and understanding your own interests, goals, and strengths.

The legendary thoroughbred trainer D. Wayne Lukas can't articulate exactly how he manages to see the potential in a yearling. He just does. Apple's revered designer Jonathan Ive can't download his taste to a computer. Ricky Gervais makes people laugh at material a machine would never dream up. Do they all use computers in their daily work lives? Unquestionably. But their genius has been to discover the ineffable strengths they possess and to spend as much time

Five paths toward employability

Humans have alternatives for how they'll work with machines. Here's a look at them in one realm: marketing.

	How you add value	Example	If this is your strategy, how do you prepare?
Step up	You may be senior management material—you're better at considering the big picture than any computer is.	A *brand manager* orchestrates all the activities required to position a brand successfully.	Get that MBA or PhD and constantly challenge yourself to gain broader perspective on your work.
Step aside	You bring strengths to the table that aren't about purely rational, codifiable cognition.	A *creative* can intuit which concept will resonate with sophisticated customers.	Develop your "multiple intelligences" beyond IQ and gain tacit knowledge through apprenticeships.
Step in	You understand how software makes routine decisions, so you monitor and modify its function and outputs.	A *pricing* expert relies on computers to optimize pricing on a daily basis and intervenes as necessary for special cases or experiments.	Pursue some STEM education and keep updating your business domain expertise.
Step narrowly	You specialize in something for which no computer program has yet been developed (although theoretically it could be).	A *"wrap advertising" specialist* has deep expertise in using vehicles as mobile billboards.	Look for a narrow niche and master it by doing the work with focus and passion.
Step forward	You build the next generation or application of smart machines—perhaps for a vendor of them.	A *digital innovator* seizes on a new way to use data to optimize some key decision, such as cable video ad buys.	Stay at the cutting edge in computer science, artificial intelligence, and analytics. Learn to spot candidates for automation.

as possible putting them to work. Machines can perform numerous ancillary tasks that would otherwise encroach on the ability of these professionals to do what they do best.

We don't want to create the impression that stepping aside is purely for artists. Senior lawyers, for example, are thoroughly versed in the law but are rarely their firms' deep-dive experts on all its fine points. They devote much of their energy to winning new work (usually the chief reason they get promoted) and acting as wise counselors to their clients. With machines digesting legal documents and suggesting courses of action and arguments, senior lawyers will have more capacity to do the rest of their job well. The same is true for many other professionals, such as senior accountants, architects, investment bankers, and consultants.

Take the realm of elder care, in which robotics manufacturers see great potential for automation. This isn't often treated as a nuanced or a particularly intellectual line of human work. We were struck, therefore, by a recent essay by the teacher, coach, and blogger Heather Plett. She wrote of her mother's palliative care provider, "She was *holding space* for us," and explained: "What does it mean to *hold space* for someone else? It means that we are willing to walk alongside another person in whatever journey they're on without judging them, making them feel inadequate, trying to fix them, or trying to impact the outcome. When we hold space for other people, we open our hearts, offer unconditional support, and let go of judgement and control."

True, hospice care is an extreme example of a situation requiring the human touch. But empathy is valuable in any setting that has customers, coworkers, and owners.

If stepping aside is your strategy, you need to focus on your uncodifiable strengths, first discovering them and then diligently working to heighten them. In the process you should identify other masters of the tacit trade you're pursuing and find ways to work with them, whether as collaborator or apprentice. You may have to develop a greater respect for the intelligences you have beyond IQ, which decades of schooling might well have devalued. These, too, can be deliberately honed—they are no more or less God-given than your capacity for calculus.

Step in

Back in 1967, having witnessed the first attempts to automate knowledge work, Peter Drucker declared of the computer: "It's a total moron." It's a lot less moronic now, but its relentless logic still occasionally arrives at decisions whose improvement wouldn't require a human genius.

Perhaps you saw a 2014 story in the *New York Times* about a man who had just changed jobs and applied to refinance his mortgage. Even though he'd had a steady government job for eight years and a steady teaching job for more than 20 years before that, he was turned down for the loan. The automated system that evaluated his application recognized that the projected payments were well within his income level, but it was smart enough to seize on a risk marker: His new career would involve a great deal more variation and uncertainty in earnings.

Or maybe that system wasn't so smart. The man was Ben Bernanke, a former chairman of the U.S. Federal Reserve, who had just signed a book contract for more than a million dollars and was headed for a lucrative stint on the lecture circuit. This is a prime example of why, when computers make decisions, we will always need people who can step in and save us from their worst tendencies.

Those capable of stepping in know how to monitor and modify the work of computers. Taxes may increasingly be done by computer, but smart accountants look out for the mistakes that automated programs—and the programs' human users—often make. Ad buying in digital marketing is almost exclusively automated these days, but only people can say when some "programmatic" buy would actually hurt the brand and how the logic behind it might be tuned.

Here you might ask, Just who is augmenting whom (or what) in this situation? It's a good moment to emphasize that in an augmentation environment, support is mutual. The human ensures that the computer is doing a good job and makes it better. This is the point being made by all those people who encourage more STEM (science, technology, engineering, and math) education. They envision a work world largely made up of stepping-in positions. But if this is your strategy, you'll also need to develop your powers of observation, translation, and human connection.

Step narrowly

This approach involves finding a specialty within your profession that wouldn't be economical to automate. In Boston, near the headquarters of Dunkin' Donuts, a reporter recently peered into "the secret world of the Dunkin' Donuts franchise kings." One of them, Gary Joyal, makes a good living (if his Rolls-Royce is any indication) by connecting buyers and sellers of Dunkin' Donuts franchises. As the *Boston Globe* put it, Joyal "uses his encyclopedic knowledge of franchisees—and often their family situations, income portfolios, and estate plans—to make himself an indispensable player for buyers and sellers alike." So far he has helped to broker half a billion dollars' worth of deals.

Could Joyal's encyclopedic knowledge be encoded in software? Probably. But no one would make enough doing so to put a Rolls in the driveway. It's just too small a category. The same is true of Claire Bustarret's work. *Johns Hopkins Magazine* reports that Bustarret "has made a career out of knowing paper like other French people know wine." Her ability to determine from a sheet's texture, feel, and fibers when and where the paper was made is extremely valuable to historians and art authenticators. Maybe what she knows could be put in a database, and her analytical techniques could be automated. But in the meantime, she would have learned more.

Those who step narrowly find such niches and burrow deep inside them. They are hedgehogs to the stepping-up foxes among us. Although most of them have the benefit of a formal education, the expertise that fuels their earning power is gained through on-the-job training—and the discipline of focus. If this is your strategy, start making a name for yourself as the person who goes a mile deep on a subject an inch wide. That won't mean you can't also have other interests, but professionally you'll have a very distinct brand. How might machines augment you? You'll build your own databases and routines for keeping current, and connect with systems that combine your very specialized output with that of others.

Step forward

Finally, stepping forward means constructing the next generation of computing and AI tools. It's still true that behind every great machine is a person—in fact, many people. Someone decides that the Dunkin' Franchise Optimizer is a bad investment, or that the application of AI to cancer drug discovery is a good one. Someone has to build the next great automated insurance-underwriting solution. Someone intuits the human need for a better system; someone identifies the part of it that can be codified; someone writes the code; and someone designs the conditions under which it will be applied.

Clearly this is a realm in which knowledge workers need strong skills in computer science, artificial intelligence, and analytics. In his book *Data-ism*, Steve Lohr offers stories of some of the people doing this work. For example, at the E. & J. Gallo Winery, an executive named Nick Dokoozlian teams up with Hendrik Hamann, a member of IBM's research staff, to find a way to harness the data required for "precision agriculture" at scale. In other words, they want to automate the painstaking craft of giving each grapevine exactly the care and feeding it needs to thrive. This isn't amateur hour. Hamann is a physicist with a thorough knowledge of IBM's prior application of networked sensors. Dokoozlian earned his doctorate in plant physiology at what Lohr informs us is the MIT of wine science—the University of California at Davis—and then taught there for 15 years. We're tempted to say that this team knows wine the way some French people know paper.

Stepping forward means bringing about machines' next level of encroachment, but it involves work that is itself highly augmented by software. A glance at Hamann's LinkedIn page is sufficient to make the point: He's been "endorsed" by contacts for his expert use of simulations, algorithms, machine learning, mathematical modeling, and more. But spotting the right next opportunity for automation requires much more than technical chops. If this is your strategy, you'll reach the top of your field if you can also think outside the box, perceive where today's computers fall short, and envision tools that don't yet exist. Someday, perhaps, even a lot of software development will be automated; but as Bill Gates recently observed, programming is "safe for now."

Why Employers Love Augmentation (or Should)

Our conversations to date with professionals in a wide range of fields—radiologists, financial advisers, teachers, architects, journalists, lawyers, accountants, marketers, and other experts of many kinds—suggest that whatever the field, any of the five steps we've just laid out is possible. Not all of them are right for a given individual, but if you can figure out which one is right for you, you'll be on your way to an augmentation strategy.

You might not get very far, however, if employers in your field don't buy in to augmentation. The world suffers from an automation mindset today, after all, because businesses have taken us down that path. Managers are always acutely aware of the downside of human employees—or, to use the technologist's favored dysphemism for them, "wetware." Henry Ford famously said, "Why is it every time I ask for a pair of hands, they come with a brain attached?"

For augmentation to work, employers must be convinced that the combination of humans and computers is better than either working alone. That realization will dawn as it becomes increasingly clear that enterprise success depends much more on constant innovation than on cost efficiency. Employers have tended to see machines and people as substitute goods: If one is more expensive, it makes sense to swap in the other. But that makes sense only under static conditions, when we can safely assume that tomorrow's tasks will be the same as today's.

Yuh-Mei Hutt told us that in her small business (Golden Lighting, a manufacturer of residential fixtures), automation has made operations much more efficient. But that means profitability depends now more than ever on the creativity of her people. Her designers need to know about trends in the interior design world and in lighting technology and must find fresh ways to pull them together. Her salespeople rely on CRM software, but their edge comes from how well they connect in person with retail buyers.

In an era of innovation, the emphasis has to be on the upside of people. They will always be the source of next-generation ideas and the element of operations that is hardest for competitors to replicate. (If you think employees today lack loyalty, you haven't noticed how fast software takes up with your rivals.) Yes, people are variable and unpredictable; capable of selfishness, boredom, and dishonesty; hard to teach and quick to tire—all things that robots are not. But with the proper augmentation, you can get the most out of the positive qualities on which they also hold a monopoly. As computerization turns everything that can be programmed into table stakes, those are the only qualities that will set you apart.

Winning a Different Kind of Race

To be sure, many of the things knowledge workers do today will soon be automated. For example, the future role of humans in financial advising isn't fully clear, but it's unlikely that those who remain in the field will have as their primary role recommending an optimal portfolio of stocks and bonds. In a recent conversation, one financial adviser seemed worried: "Our advice to clients isn't fully automated yet," he said, "but it's feeling more and more robotic. My comments to clients are increasingly supposed to follow a script, and we are strongly encouraged to move clients into the use of these online tools." He expressed his biggest fear outright: "I'm thinking that over time they will phase us out altogether." But the next words out of his mouth more than hinted at his salvation: "Reading scripts is obviously something a computer can do; convincing a client to invest more money requires some more skills. I'm already often more of a psychiatrist than a stockbroker."

That's not a step down. It's at least a step aside, and probably a step up. The adviser and his firm need only to see it that way and then build on it. For the foreseeable future, prompting savers and investors to make wiser financial choices will not be an automated task.

The strategy that will work in the long term, for employers and the employed, is to view smart machines as our partners and collaborators in knowledge work. By emphasizing augmentation, we can remove the threat of automation and turn the race with the machine into a relay rather than a dash. Those who are able to smoothly transfer the baton to and from a computer will be the winners.

Originally published in June 2015. Reprint R1506C

About the Contributors

DOMINIC BARTON is the global managing director of McKinsey & Company and a trustee of the Brookings Institution.

DENNIS CAREY is vice chairman of Korn Ferry, where he specializes in CEO and board director recruitment. He is coauthor (with Ram Charan and Michael Useem) of *Boards That Lead* (Harvard Business Review Press, 2014).

RAM CHARAN is a business adviser to CEOs and corporate boards. He is coauthor (with Dennis Carey and Michael Useem) of *Boards That Lead* (Harvard Business Review Press, 2014).

SANGEET PAUL CHOUDARY is the founder and CEO of Platform Thinking Labs and an entrepreneur-in-residence at INSEAD. He is the author (with Marshall W. Van Alstyne and Geoffrey G. Parker) of *Platform Revolution* (W.W. Norton & Company, 2016).

CLAYTON M. CHRISTENSEN is the Kim B. Clark Professor of Business Administration at Harvard Business School.

ROB CROSS is a professor of management at the University of Virginia's McIntire School of Commerce and a coauthor of *The Hidden Power of Social Networks*.

THOMAS H. DAVENPORT is a distinguished professor at Babson College, a research fellow at the MIT Center for Digital Business, and a senior adviser to Deloitte Analytics. He is the author (with Julia Kirby) of *Only Humans Need Apply: Winners and Losers in the Age of Smart Machines*.

VIJAY GOVINDARAJAN is the Coxe Distinguished Professor at Tuck School of Business at Dartmouth and a Marvin Bower Fellow at Harvard Business School. He is the lead author of *Reverse Innovation* (Harvard Business Review Press, 2012).

ADAM GRANT is a professor of management and psychology at Wharton and the author of *Give and Take* and *Originals*.

ADI IGNATIUS is Editor in Chief of *Harvard Business Review*.

JULIA KIRBY was an HBR editor at large. She is the author (with Thomas H. Davenport) of *Only Humans Need Apply: Winners and Losers in the Age of Smart Machines*.

JON KLEINBERG is a professor of computer science at Cornell University and the coauthor of the textbooks *Algorithm Design* (with Éva Tardos) and *Networks, Crowds, and Markets* (with David Easley).

MICHAEL LUCA is an assistant professor of business administration at Harvard Business School.

LINDSAY A. MARTIN is the executive director of innovation and an adviser at the Institute for Healthcare Improvement.

PATRICIA A. McDONALD is Intel's vice president of human resources and the director of the Intel Talent Organization.

RORY McDONALD is an assistant professor at Harvard Business School.

ROBERT S. MECKLENBURG, MD, is the medical director of the Center for Health Care Solutions at Virginia Mason Medical Center.

ERIN MEYER is a professor and the program director for Managing Global Virtual Teams at INSEAD. She is the author of *The Culture Map: Breaking Through the Invisible Boundaries of Global Business*.

SENDHIL MULLAINATHAN is a professor of economics at Harvard University and the coauthor (with Eldar Shafir) of *Scarcity: Why Having Too Little Means So Much*.

INDRA NOOYI is chairman and CEO of PepsiCo.

GEOFFREY G. PARKER is a professor of management science at Tulane University and is a fellow at the MIT Center for Digital Business.

As of July 2016, he is a professor of engineering at Dartmouth College. He is the author (with Marshall W. Van Alstyne and Sangeet Paul Choudary) of *Platform Revolution* (W.W. Norton & Company, 2016).

MICHAEL RAYNOR is a director at Deloitte Consulting LLP.

REB REBELE is a research fellow in the Wharton People Analytics initiative at the University of Pennsylvania.

MARSHALL W. VAN ALSTYNE is a professor and chair of the information systems department at Boston University and a fellow at the MIT Initiative on the Digital Economy. He is the author (with Geoffrey G. Parker and Sangeet Paul Choudary) of *Platform Revolution* (W.W. Norton & Company, 2016).

ADAM WAYTZ is an associate professor of management and organizations at Northwestern University's Kellogg School of Management.

AMOS WINTER is the Robert N. Noyce Career Development Assistant Professor and the director of the Global Engineering and Research Laboratory in the department of mechanical engineering at the Massachusetts Institute of Technology.

Index

The most important management ideas all in one place.

We hope you enjoyed this HBR's 10 Must Reads book. Now, you can get even more with HBR's 10 Must Reads Boxed Set. From books on leadership and strategy to managing yourself and others, this 6-book collection delivers articles on the most essential business topics to help you succeed.

HBR's 10 Must Reads Series

The HBR's 10 Must Reads Series is the definitive collection of ideas and best practices on our most sought-after topics from the best minds in business.

- The Essentials
- Leadership
- Strategy
- Managing People
- Managing Yourself
- Collaboration
- Communication
- Making Smart Decisions
- Teams
- Innovation
- Strategic Marketing
- Change Management

New Ideas and Resources to Help You Achieve Even More with
Harvard Business Review

EASIER, SMARTER, PERSONALIZED

As a business executive, you are called upon to lead;
Harvard Business Review **provides the tools to keep you ahead, including the beautifully redesigned HBR.org. Imagine ...**

- On-demand access to more than 4,000 articles, interviews, features, and ideas in HBR.org's reimagined archive.

- Just-published articles **on topics you choose** rushed to your personalized My Library

- Seamless sharing of content with your colleagues.

Now, don't just imagine it. Employ it!

TO SEE ALL A SUBSCRIPTION INCLUDES, GO TO:
hbr.org/subscribe